Is Counselling Training for You?

IS COUNSELLING TRAINING FOR YOU?

Val Potter

sheldonPRESS

First published in Great Britain in 1997 by
Sheldon Press, SPCK, Marylebone Road, London NW1 4DU

The author and publisher would like to thank the British
Association for Counselling for granting permission to reproduce
material from the following documents:

The BAC Code of Ethics and Practice for Counsellors, May 1996,
BAC.
'The BAC Scheme for Recognition of Counsellor Training Courses,
Guidelines for Client Work, Training Placements and Supervision
in Counsellor Training Courses', in *Counselling*, February 1996,
BAC.

British Association for Counselling Codes are regularly updated
and readers are advised to check that they are current.

British Library Cataloguing-in-Publication Data
A catalogue record for this book is available from the British
Library

ISBN 0–85969–746–0

Photoset by Deltatype Ltd, Birkenhead, Merseyside
Printed in Great Britain by Biddles Ltd, Guildford and King's Lynn

To John

| *Contents*

| *Acknowledgements*

First I want to thank John, my dear husband, who has inspired me with his own skill in writing, been my first, clear-eyed reader and kept the home fires burning while I slaved over a hot word processor. Thanks, John; it is your turn now. Thanks to Joanna Moriarty, publisher, Sheldon Press, who asked me to write this book and has always been there to provide me with help and encouragement when I began to run out of steam. I am grateful to several of my valued colleagues and friends, who have provided their professional knowledge and experience in various ways. Thank you, Mary-Anne Coate, Shirley Frost, Lesley Murdin and Moyra Peters. For Chapter 6: Choosing an Approach, I drew on Richard Nelson-Jones' book *The Theory and Practice of Counselling* (Cassell, 1995) for background information on approaches with which I am less familiar. I commend his thorough and valuable work in setting out such a wide range of counselling approaches so clearly. My next thank you is for Jennifer Jones, who expertly transcribed the interviews in Chapter 2.

Finally, my thanks to Westminster Pastoral Foundation for giving me the opportunity to teach their short course 'Is Counsellor Training for You?'; one of many creative opportunities they have given to me. Thank you to Janet Lake, who devised the course and special thanks to all the participants in 'Is Counsellor Training for You?' over the years. Your questions and discussions have shaped this book. I hope that you enjoy the result.

Val Potter

1
Is Counselling Training for You?

You have picked up this book because this question interests you in some way. Perhaps you are thinking about embarking on counsellor training, or you may already be in training and be looking for a book which will help you to make the most of your course. Over twenty years as a counselling trainer I have worked with many students, from beginners to advanced trainees. This book is based on the questions they have raised, on what they have taught me, as well as on my own counselling experience. It is designed as a guidebook to help you to discover whether you want to become a counsellor and, if you do, how to go about it.

If you do decide to become an explorer, to find out whether counsellor training is for you, what is it like to enter the world of counselling today? Join me now as I meet a group of people in a training room. Twenty of them have come together to participate in a course called 'Is Counsellor Training for You?'[1] They are introducing themselves to me and to my husband, who are their trainers for this weekend, and to each other.

> I am a nurse. I get most satisfaction in my work from forming a good relationship with my patients. I want to learn counselling skills to help me to be better at my job.

> I run my own business. It is successful, and I am financially secure, but I want to feel that I am doing something where the focus is not making money, something which, in a small way, makes the world a better place.

> I work in computers. I went through a bad patch five years ago and a counsellor helped me to get through it. I would like to be able to do for other people what he did for me.

> I work in the arts. I have worked on many radio programmes which explore the knotty issues of everyday life. I listen to people talking about the events which have shaped their lives and I want to be able to help them to deal with them, rather than just report their experiences.

As I listen to them, I think back over my 15 years of working on this course, meeting groups of people, all coming with the question at the head of this chapter. Over the years the make-up of the groups has changed. In the beginning fewer participants were in paid employment, and those who were employed were likely to be working in the caring professions. Most counsellors then were working voluntarily, putting in a few hours a week in their local community, or were in work which involved counselling. Those in the groups I meet today probably know that there are many opportunities in counselling now, both paid and voluntary. If they stay the course they will enter an occupation which is becoming increasingly professionalized and regulated, but is still changing and forming.

As we move into the course it is clear that many of the participants know something about counselling already. Some of them have sought counselling for themselves. Most have read articles in the press or seen TV documentaries. One of the group has brought with her an article which is less than complimentary about counsellors and counselling. If you are thinking of becoming a counsellor it is important that you are not naive and that you do not have an unrealistic picture that you will make a fortune, that you will be able to help everyone, or that everyone will love you. Working as a counsellor will not give you a peaceful retreat from the rat race, and becoming a counsellor is a long and demanding process.

If you become a counsellor you will also discover that you may not be left to work quietly in a consulting room. Like every other profession, counselling is under scrutiny. We have to be ready to face hard questioning. Recently I sat in a studio, taking part in a radio phone-in. The questions came thick and fast. What is counselling? Does counselling work? I talked to a retired policeman, who was sceptical about 'all this politically correct stuff'. 'The police are tough, we can cope with anything,' was his line. 'All this counselling will make the emergency services soft. Then how will they cope?' Then I listened to a businessman who had thought that he could cope with anything, until his wife left him and he fell apart. 'I went to a counsellor because I was desperate, and I didn't know what to do,' he said. 'My counsellor saved my life.' He had no doubt that counselling works.

As the programme went on the presenter asked me how someone can know whether a counsellor they see is properly qualified for the work. We must all have heard frightening stories told by people who are angry and hurt, because they feel that they have not received a professional standard of care from a counsellor. Of course they are news because they are rare, but we cannot afford to be complacent about them. I gave the listeners to the phone-in some information about how to find a properly qualified counsellor.

There are three basic questions at the heart of the public debate:

- What is counselling?
- Are counsellors properly trained and do they know what they are doing?
- How do I know that counselling is any good; that it actually helps?

The reason that the phone-in was happening, along with a lot of other media interest, is that counselling and counsellors are to be found everywhere. This is a recent phenomenon. Children witness a violent event. Counsellors are brought in to help them and their families. Members of the emergency services deal with a major disaster. They are traumatized by what they see and hear, and are provided with counselling to help them to recover. This is the public face of the counselling profession, but in workplaces, colleges, doctors' surgeries, at major public events and in small local voluntary counselling centres – wherever there are people who need someone who will help them to make sense of their experiences, and to work out what to do with their lives – counsellors are quietly at work, providing a confidential place to talk and bringing their skilled attention to the task. In addition there are many people in other walks of life who undertake training in counselling skills to help them to be better at their job. Some are in the 'helping professions', others are in a range of other occupations. All share a need to be able to deal with people with sensitivity and care, and to understand more about what 'makes them tick'.

In response to the growing demand for counsellors and counselling expertise, counselling training courses are proliferating. Their quality varies enormously. The membership of the British Association for Counselling (BAC), the organization which promotes and represents counselling and counsellors, is growing by 10 per cent or more a year. Those of us who work in counsellor training sometimes ask ourselves if we are training too many people. Will there be enough work to go round? I do not know the answer to that question, but I do know that if there is increased competition for counselling work those who are best prepared, best trained, best qualified and with a wide range of experience are most likely to succeed.

So, if your answer to the question 'Is counsellor training for you?' might be 'Yes', come and find out if you have what it takes to join us. Like all good counsellor training, the book invites your active involvement, wherever possible. You do not have to join in the exercises, if for some reason you feel you would rather not, but experience tells me that the more that you are willing to take risks and try things out, the more you will get from the experience. I hope that you are interested enough to read on. I hope you will find that, whether or not you finally decide that you want to be a counsellor, the journey of discovery is interesting in itself.

2
On Being a Counsellor

Before you start to explore whether counsellor training might be for you, come with me to meet three experienced counsellors and to hear them talk about their work. When I talked to them I had some particular questions in mind. What kind of person is drawn to be a counsellor? What is it like to work as a counsellor? What particular satisfactions do counsellors get from their work? I make some observations at the end of the chapter, but they are by no means conclusive. I wonder what you notice as you read these interviews. I have not revealed the identity of the interviewees, so that they are free to talk about their work and their lives.

Counselling in the Voluntary Sector

The first counsellor works in a busy centre which houses a comprehensive counselling service (individual, couple and group counselling), and offers counsellor training in a large town in the south east. The town is on a main rail route within commuting distance of London and has seen an influx of young families attracted by access both to the nearby countryside and to work in the London area. The centre was founded in the early 1970s by a group of enthusiastic and energetic volunteers, who recognized the need for counsellors to serve a rapidly growing population, who were usually having to manage their lives without the day-to-day support of their wider families. The counselling service is based in a semi-detached house near the rail station and five minutes' walk from the town centre. From the outside the only thing which distinguishes it from the other tidy houses in the street is a plaque with the name of the centre on the wall next to the main door. Inside, the offices are on the ground floor, and there are two more floors, each with three counselling rooms, and a waiting area. The counselling rooms are comfortable and soundproof, but not luxurious. The centre is a hive of activity for five and a half days a week. The counselling service still relies on the work of a team of around 30 dedicated volunteer counsellors. Some have other work and give a few hours a week; others work mainly here.

We are about to meet a counsellor who has been a mainstay of this centre from the beginning. She sits in front of me now leaning forward and talking animatedly, in a way which is characteristic of her. She enjoys conversation and has a lively curiosity, which often leads her to look beneath the surface of the obvious. Here she is, talking about her work.

I started to train as a counsellor in 1975. I was just finishing a degree in social studies and I was doing a hospital social work placement at a local psychiatric hospital. A group called the Counselling Network had just formed locally and I went along to a meeting, because I was interested in finding out about counselling. At the meeting were a group of people who were talking about setting up a counselling service in the town. I was really excited by the idea. I had enjoyed the casework part of my social studies placements, but I didn't like the bureaucracy of social work; all the paperwork and form-filling. So I talked to them and they explained how I could do an introductory course in London, and that's how I started.

I have been doing individual counselling for a number of years, but last year I stopped doing that and decided to focus on work with couples and groups. I did a course in couples work about ten years ago. I am seeing about four couples at any one time now, and I run two therapy groups. I have done all this work for the counselling centre that we set up in the 1970s. I get paid for the group conducting and I get an honorarium each year for the rest of the counselling. I suppose that when I was doing individual work the most I was paid was £900 to £1,000 in a year. I was seeing six individuals and three couples a week, but when I think of it, there are seven people in each of the groups, and so, although I only work for a day and an evening now, I have 22 people I see in a week. That's a lot of people to think about, but in the groups people help each other. There are things that happen in a group that can never happen in individual counselling. For instance one of the group members may say to another, 'You are telling us a sad story and you are smiling.' You have several people commenting on what they see. I have become really excited recently about the possibilities of groups. I did some group-work training and I have supervision from a group psychotherapist.

I started counselling when my youngest child was just starting secondary school. In those years when the children were adolescents, I am sure that I coped with them in a very different way than I would have if I had not had any understanding of human development. I was understanding more about my life at that time and about my relationships with my parents. That helped me to relate to my children as they grew up, and to accept them for the different people that they are. I relate to them in a different way from the way my parents related to me.

I learned more about myself too, and that strengthened me. I feel that I am more my own person, rather than being how other people expect me to be. That was important, because I grew up with a great need to be what my parents expected. I can't imagine what kind of person I would be if I had not got into counselling. I think that I would have probably gone into social work. I knew that I did not want to go back into nursing, which was what I had originally trained for. If I had been a social worker I would probably just have done the job, because I needed to do something, and I wanted to do something for other people, but counselling has helped me to get a lot for myself too. All the time that I have been in counselling I have been developing my self-knowledge and my self-worth, and that seems to me to be a much better balance. In nursing I didn't get anything, I was just there to give.

At the beginning I think that it helped that I was working voluntarily, because I was doing something new, and it took me quite a long time to feel that I was worth any payment. It makes a difference that I was working with other people, helping to establish a counselling centre. At the beginning we were all doing something together that we believed in, and there was no way that we could carry on the ideal of the organization – which was to provide counselling for everyone, regardless of their ability to pay – if we had been paid. I was on the executive of the counselling centre too, and I did a stint as training manager. I have always felt involved. I look after the counsellors' library. I feel that I am contributing to the ideal of what I always wanted it to be, which is a place where counsellors support each other, where there is always someone there if you come out from having a difficult session. I can't imagine just doing counselling alone, and having individual supervision, and not having the support of a group. I don't think that I could have done that. The centre may not pay us, but it gives us a lot. We have insurance cover; specialized regular supervision for individual work and couples work; and in-service training, all free. Even the coffee is free.

There have been difficult times of course, times when I have had several difficult clients, and times when I have wondered if I am really up to the job, and even had a kind of longing to be free from it. But when I am in a supervision group with my colleagues I know that we all go through that, and you just have to ask for their support to help you in the difficult times.

Counselling has changed quite a lot since the time that I first became involved. The organization that I work for has grown tenfold since that time. That has entailed a great deal more organization, more rules, and the need to get more certificates and diplomas all the time. They are the most obvious changes. I think that making things more formal has been good. In the beginning you know, we were very much novices, and then the people who were not able to move on and who didn't do extra training dropped out.

Counselling is more in the public eye now but it is quite difficult for me to know how the public see us. In the early days I never told anyone that I was a counsellor. That was partly my own insecurity – I didn't want to be asked any questions that I could not answer – and it was partly that counselling was not very accepted. I think that has changed very much, and now I think there is not the same stigma on those who go for counselling. There is not such a strong expectation that people should try to cope with everything by themselves. There are not many people who ask me about my work and if they do ask me what I do and I tell them, they usually say 'I quite admire you for doing that' or 'I don't think that I could do that', as though it is something a bit strange. Possibly being a counsellor sets me apart from other people sometimes, but I have no idea whether I wish to set myself apart, or whether I am being set apart. I do not know. That is interesting. I will think about it.

This counsellor evokes the excitement of being a pioneer; one of a close-knit group who learned together, discovered new aspects of themselves and worked to develop training and counselling in their area. For her counselling is much more than a job, it is a way of life. Like many counsellors she is excited by the prospect of developing her skills and finding new ways to apply them. She does not take her motivation and feelings for granted; rather she enjoys finding questions for reflection. She wonders whether her experience of feeling set apart from some other people because of her work is something which others do to her, or something which she has chosen, because it is what she wishes to happen, and she stores this away for further thought. Many counselling services in the voluntary sector are staffed by counsellors who accept the lack of material rewards, because they feel that the work enriches their lives in so many other ways.

Counselling in a General Medical Practice

Our next port of call is a busy health centre, which houses a multi-disciplinary team of nurses, doctors and counsellors. It is one of a number of such centres which meet the primary health care needs of a large town. Looking around the waiting room it is not obvious which patients have come for which service. Patients are referred for counselling by the doctors in the practice, if they feel that this treatment may benefit them. The counsellor I have come to meet had a great deal of experience of working in a counselling centre, seeing clients for open-ended work before she took up her work in the health centre, doing short-term counselling. She is friendly and animated, and has an air of enjoying life to the full. She combines down-to-earth practicality with a fine awareness of the absurdities of life. The two qualities combined give her a true sense of proportion. Here she is, talking about her work.

When people ask me how I got into counselling in the first place, my standard answer, which is true, although it may sound flippant, is that people used to tell me their life history and I didn't know what to do with it, except go home and worry about it. Then a counselling course was started in the village that I lived in, and I had friends who had started the course. They would say, 'You know, you ought to come along to this, you'd really enjoy it.' I thought, 'Oh well, maybe I will', and so I went along and it was right for me. I learned that I didn't have to take people's problems home with me, that they eventually learned how to deal with them, and I didn't have to do it for them. That's been good for me. I've enjoyed it enormously and still carry that with me as being the best thing I ever learned from counselling.

These days I do some of my counselling in a GP surgery. I got into it by accident really. The surgery approached the organization I work for as a counsellor. They wanted some counsellors who were interested in working in the practice to come along for an exploratory interview. They wanted two people to do a job-share, so a colleague and I went along, and we came out of the interview and looked at each other and I said, 'I think we've got a job' – which we had. We each did two three-hour clinics, making twelve hours in total for the practice. Now that for me has felt quite difficult, because it meant that you were taking clients for 50-minute sessions one, two, three, straight after each other. The doctors' idea was that you could do your notes in the ten minutes in between; never mind the fact that you might want to have a coffee or go to the loo. Of course, that is the way that doctors work. I did eventually get into it, but my anxiety level was pretty high when I started. The other thing was that they were pretty strict that it was going to be very short-term – six weeks maximum – which was a great contrast to the open-ended work that I had done before.

I'd had some training in short-term fixed focus counselling, but there had not been a lot of opportunity to practise it at the organization in which I'd worked. Usually I would have seen people for probably anything between a year and two years and there was quite a contrast. I knew how to do brief focused work in theory and I had already had a couple of clients who were on a 12-week contract, but I had not done anything quite so short-term until I began at the surgery.

The biggest difference between short-term and long-term work is that in short-term work you have really to focus down. You can't be as wide-ranging, because there isn't the time, and it feels to me that you need to be very responsible about what you work on, because to open cans of worms for someone you can only see for six sessions could be actually quite dangerous, unless you do it very carefully, and it feels to me that not to do it carefully would be irresponsible. That to me is the pressure of working short-term. I really like to get some background information about the client's childhood, that to me is important, because it helps me to see what they might project into their relationship with me. I need to know what they are transferring from past relationships on to their relationship with me, but I don't work with it directly, as I would in longer-term work. It's important to be aware of it and not just unwittingly fall into it, which I think might be a possibility if I didn't have the background. Now I understand that other counsellors can do it differently, but that's my way.

In the practice the doctors refer patients if they think that counselling might help them, but we do have a choice about working with them. We don't rely only on straightforward doctor referral. We have asked the doctors not to give us whole masses of information, just to say why they think that this person should have counselling, and tell us about the medication that the patient is on, and any side effects it might have. I think we're quite fortunate in our surgery, we don't get many inappropriate referrals – we really don't. Sometimes we can see somebody, and in the first session we feel that this may not be for them, and maybe they should be referred on, but some people just need six hours of someone listening to them – and whilst that might not feel quite as rewarding to us as counsellors in some ways, in the sense that we are not going to see much of any movement, it may be just what they need.

I think the greatest stress for me is the fact that you're mindful of the waiting list. There are always people waiting to be seen. You need to use your time productively. During the summer months when people are on holiday, what tends to happen is that you fill the spaces in your schedule with new clients, but you still have to be mindful of the ones who are away. Add to that the fact that you might be seeing some couples, and you can see that although in theory you're holding six people, in practice you could be holding a dozen, and that does feel quite a strain sometimes. You have to hold a lot of information, and keep in touch with a lot of feelings in your own mind, so that you're ready when they come for the next session to get on quickly – you can't spend time catching up, as you can with someone long-term.

As I have said, I see couples too at the surgery, and some families, and on a couple of occasions I've seen mothers and daughters. I trained in couples' counselling as well as individual counselling. I think that short-term work is best done by an experienced counsellor, but I'm aware that I've been on courses where there are people who don't have the sort of background that I have, and the 20 years of service that I have, and they seem quite okay with what they're doing. I do know that for me, and for other counsellors I have spoken to, the psychodynamic training[1] and experience has been invaluable, because you have a broader view of the ways in which you can help clients, and you know when to leave things alone in this short-term work. All the time you're doing this swift thinking, you're aware of other things going on that might be pursued, but you put them to one side and stick to the focus. When it comes to doing the resumé on the last session, sometimes you can bring some of the other issues forward, and register that they are around. Sometimes it is important to be open and say, 'I can understand that this issue is very difficult, and that it has been a problem for a long time, but in six weeks it does not feel appropriate to me to delve into these things, although at some point they may need to be dealt with.' So I know and they know that it's there and that I have picked it up. We are both aware of it, but I want to help them to put clear edges around what can be worked with in six weeks and what needs long-term work.

It's quite interesting you know, when I think about doing that. I have always worked psychodynamically, but I have had a fairly pragmatic view of it and maybe that pragmatism is quite useful if you're working in a surgery where it all comes – emergencies, referrals, long-term personality problems; issues as varied and as numerous as the number of people you see. I think my fairly pragmatic approach – that people have to live; they have to get on with their jobs; they have to deal with having children, bringing them up; doing all the things they need to do to survive – I think perhaps for me that's been possibly the most gratifying thing in working at the surgery, that they just get a little something that actually means they can carry on. I find that very satisfying. So maybe I'm saying that if you don't have this sort of philosophy and the feeling that it is important to think about people living in the real world, not just living in the counselling world, you might not get the same satisfaction from this work, or be able to make it as helpful and as useful to the client as possible. That's my personal view.

It's quite interesting really, because when I'm working long-term, I like to see how people sort of grow physically taller. I thought that wouldn't be possible in six weeks. I was quite sceptical about it initially. Now I think that people can still grow in short-term work, but they need to have a reasonable amount of ego strength in order to feel that they can make use of such a short period of time. They need to believe that they can actually find some solutions to their own problems. If everything devastates them and their lifetime's input has been minimal, their ego strength is then also minimal. They're going to find it hard to believe that they can do anything. It is important that they are not so battered and bruised and 'war weary' that they can't find much strength in themselves. It need only be minimal, need only be that they recognize that they don't have much, but it's important that they can look at themselves and see themselves reasonably realistically.

This counsellor is very clear about the differences between long-term and short-term work with clients. She raises the interesting question of whether you need to be an experienced counsellor in order to be 'fast enough on your psychological feet' for short-term work. As she describes it, her short-term clients may only focus on a small part of their experience, but she keeps in mind their background, their psychological resources and the other factors which affect the way she counsels them. She knows that not all of these factors can be dealt with short-term, but recognizes that it is important to take them into account. She knows her own strengths as a counsellor and talks about the way she uses her pragmatism to anchor herself and her work to the necessary preoccupations of everyday life. She raises an important dimension of work in an interdisciplinary team: relationships between the counsellors and the other members of the team. In the practice in which she works, the doctors listen to the counsellors and trust them to make decisions about how to work with their patients in counselling. I am sure that it makes a great difference to the patients who come for counselling to know that the team at the health centre are working together to give them appropriate help for their problems.

Counselling in Private Practice

Our last visit is to a house in an inner-city area. The counsellor I have come to talk to lives here, and uses a room in his house as a consulting room for his private practice. The room is light, airy and private. This counsellor is also a very experienced practitioner. He is serious and thoughtful, but not 'heavy'. I would think that he treats the issues brought to him by his clients with great care and respect. He feels calm and reliable and this room is an oasis of quiet in a noisy, busy part of the city. I ask him how he first became interested in counselling.

When I was in my late 20s I was having some relationship difficulties, and an ex-girlfriend of mine, who I was breaking up with, suggested that we should try a kind of humanistic psychotherapy which was quite big at the time. There was body work and drop-in groups, all that sort of stuff, encounter groups, and so on. She encouraged me to start dabbling and so initially, I guess, I just went into it for myself, and dabbled for some years. In retrospect I can see that it was quite helpful, because I was quite withdrawn, and quite a private character, so even though I don't use that methodology at all now, at the time it helped me. Maybe anything would be exactly what you need, if you can make use of it. I'm not saying another method couldn't have helped me, but that did make me start to express myself. I mean it was quite group-orientated, workshop-orientated, all that cathartic stuff, letting your feelings out – it did help me to start coming out of myself.

I was a school teacher at the time and not enjoying it at all. I wanted to do something else, and having done this sort of stuff for four or five years, I thought that if I trained to be a counsellor, it would be a way of getting out of teaching. Again in retrospect I would now say it was a wish for some proper intensive therapy on myself. I wanted growth for myself which I put into the idea of doing a training. One of my things at the moment is that so many people are coming into counselling because they think anybody can do it. They think, 'I don't want to be a manager or I don't want to be a this – I'll train to be a counsellor.' The market is flooded with counselling and some very shabby counsellors, not just some, a lot I think.

In some ways counselling is easier than being a teacher, in the sense that, particularly if you're in private practice as I am, there is some control of who you see and who you don't see, some choice. If you're in another setting like teaching, then you have to take whoever appears on the scene and you have to work through, or not necessarily work through the difficulties, but face them day after day.

In another way, I've been doing this work now for 13 years, and I actually find the work much more difficult in one sense than I did at the start, because I see more. I've got less of the sort of arrogance that

I had. I don't know if arrogance is the right word, but I see it as arrogance. At the time when I started out, my attitude would be, 'Well, a psychiatrist couldn't help these people, but all they need is to be talked to as a real person and that would help them.' I had the idea that all people needed was a really good listening ear and I was that ear. But actually the work gets, I think, increasingly difficult, as it gets deeper. I'm not just saying that in a sort of pseudo-modesty way; it does actually get more difficult. I see more possibilities in it, that it's not just about being a listening ear, there's so much more that I can offer, and I am more aware of the limitations of what I can actually do. Indeed that there are some people who it's dangerous to work with at all. I never had that idea when I first started out, that somebody had sorted out some sort of a life for themselves and actually to go to some therapy or counselling would be too provocative and they might end up in a worse place than before; that it might actually be dangerous, and leave their life worse than it was before. I'm much more aware of that now.

I get angry about shabby counsellors, because I think some people take on this idea too lightly. I've come across them through my work as a supervisor, and from what I hear from clients who've been in other therapies. Some of the stuff one hears about is really very frightening. I had someone, as an example, who had come to me through work, for supervision to do with his work. He was doing a counsellor training. The training required him to be in counselling so he started seeing somebody for counselling. He said to this counsellor, 'I'll also need supervision for this course' and the counsellor said, 'I can do that too. We'll do the counselling session, then we'll have a cup of tea and then do the supervision.' This sort of stuff frightens me.

I work mostly in private practice now, although I do some staff groups and that sort of thing for organizations. I was doing quite a lot of work in organizations, in a teaching capacity, teaching counselling and so on, and I wanted to build something up for myself, so I made that a priority a few years ago. It just gives me that sense of freedom – today, for instance, the sun was shining and I had some time so I sat and read for a while. I have a varied working week; I work with people one-to-one and in groups, I supervise, I work with staff groups and I'm also studying part-time at the moment.

I did my first training in individual work, which was a humanistic training, and then I did a training for group work, and both of them were quite extensive trainings. The individual training was four years of about eight hours a week, and the group training was five years and that again was seven or eight hours a week. I gave about ten years to training and I'm still thinking of doing more. I think that I regret not throwing myself into the training deeply enough. My wife's doing a psychotherapeutic training at the moment. I see the amount of reading she has to do – she really studies for it. She prepares everything carefully, whereas I would always do the minimum, skim-read a paper, that kind of thing. I watch her and I see the amount she's actually got out of it because of what she's put into it – so I have that regret, that I didn't put enough into my training.

The most satisfying thing about this work is when I see people's lives change for the better. I really do think that this work is a privilege, in the sense that you get entry into people's lives in such an amazing way. Last week I did two interviews and they were people I would never normally come across. One bloke in particular who looked a bit funny – literally – he'd be the sort of man I might have crossed the road to avoid at one time, but to end up talking with him and to find out what he was actually like, was an extraordinary experience. There's all of that which is on the positive side; people's complexities, their amazing lives, all of that. The downside is what I'll loosely call the 'difficult' clients. For instance, clients that attack for whatever reason. To withstand that can be difficult and some of it can be very disturbing to live with. A few times I have been traumatized by things that have happened, by some very powerful events, and in that situation I've found my supervision invaluable. I go to supervision each week. I imagine I'll do that for ever, because I find that there is a lot to contain, particularly when something traumatic happens.

Many counsellors start by seeking some kind of therapeutic help to deal with issues in their own lives. When this is effective, and they are able to make the desired changes, this success forms the foundation of their faith in the work they do. This counsellor paints a clear picture of some of the pleasures and pains of private practice. It is good to be able to choose the work you do and to work flexible hours which suit you, but you take on a good deal of responsibility, and the effects of that can sometimes be traumatic. One of the purposes of counselling is to enable people to get in touch with their feelings and to express them more freely. Being on the receiving end of powerfully expressed feelings is not always comfortable. It is important for counsellors to have an active social conscience and a well-developed sense of personal responsibility, if they are to maintain high ethical standards in their work. This counsellor talks about his anger with 'shabby' practice, and of his awareness of the limits of what he can do and who he can help. This sense of proportion is vital to protect clients from the inflated claims and confusing practices of counsellors like the one described in this interview, who sees no difficulty in taking on the two very different roles of counsellor and supervisor with the same person.

On Becoming a Counsellor

I have been aware, in talking to these three counsellors, that there are some characteristics that they share. I think that they are to be found in all the counsellors I know. All have a need to try to know and understand themselves better. If they react in a certain way, they are likely to wonder why. 'Why might I choose work which seems to set me apart?' the first counsellor asks herself. 'Is it because it suits me in some way, or is it an unfortunate by-product of the work?' All three counsellors do not settle for an easy life. They have made considerable sacrifices in time and money to train for their work and all are willing to take on the risks of being responsible for difficult cases. They both stretch themselves and maintain a keen awareness of the proper limits of the work they do. I came away from my meeting with each of them with the feeling that each of them knows how hard and painful life can be. They have seen and heard a lot about the suffering of others. At the same time they have a faith that people can change and grow, not least through painful experience, and that life is worth the struggle because of the deep satisfactions it can offer.

If you are intrigued and excited by what the counsellors have to say, now is the time to find out whether you have what it takes to join them. Counsellors are seekers after truth, never satisfied with ready-made answers, as you have already discovered, so as you set out to read the rest of this book, try to do so with your mind open to new ways of looking at yourself and at this world of counselling.

3
The Qualities of a Good Counsellor

I am about to show a video to a group of students. They have spent six months taking their first steps to acquire counselling skills; they have struggled to be sensitive, to listen, to empathize with their fellow students as they practise counselling them in role-play exercises. Now I explain that the ageing film that they are about to see shows a young woman, Gloria,[1] boldly going where no woman has gone before, into the consulting rooms of three famous therapists. We will see her take her concerns to Carl Rogers, founder of 'person-centred therapy', to Fritz Perls, originator of 'gestalt therapy', and to Arthur Ellis, patriarch of 'rational emotive therapy'.

My students look like Israelites who have been wandering in the wilderness and have just had their first glimpse of the promised land. Now they will discover how to do it; they will learn the secret of being a good counsellor. A reverent hush descends as the rather old and fuzzy images appear and Gloria shakes hands with Dr Carl Rogers. We watch as she tells Dr Rogers that she would have liked to have had a father like him and he replies that he is sure she would have been a nice daughter. She moves on to Dr Perls, who smokes non-stop and spills ash down his three-piece suit. He insists that she is angry with him; points out that she is tapping her foot and urges her to 'do it more' and then to say, 'I am angry with you, Fritz.' Gloria's smile fades and she seems uncomfortable. It is with a look of distinct apprehension that she enters Dr Ellis' consulting room. He talks much more than the other two, and is full of explanations, rules and instructions. Gloria listens attentively, clearly impressed by him.

As our heroine walks out of her last consulting room I set the video to 'pause' before the last scene where she comments on her experiences. First I want to know what the students think. 'Have you discovered what makes a good counsellor?' I ask. 'Dr Rogers has such empathy,' someone says. 'Did you notice that he never took his eyes off Gloria, and how gentle his voice is? I would love to take my problems to him. I am sure he would understand.' 'I don't like Dr Perls,' volunteers another student. There is a murmur of agreement. 'He kept on at her. Did you see how uncomfortable she looked? I bet she would never go back to him again.' They temporarily agree to strike off Dr Perls and turn their attention to Dr Ellis. 'Too bossy,' they decide.

It looks as if they have reached agreement, when someone ventures: 'Perhaps a counsellor can be too nice?' The students remember how Dr Perls drew Gloria's attention to some darker feelings, which had not emerged with Dr Rogers. As the discussion continues the earlier certainties fade. For every argument there is a counter-argument. We return to the video to see if Gloria can help us. 'Well,' she is saying, 'I liked Dr Rogers. He is a really nice person. Dr Ellis is clever. Dr Perls made me angry, but I feel I got further with him. I think he is the one I would be most likely to go to again.'

Of course many people have benefited from counselling inspired by all these great pioneers and their followers. We all owe them a great debt. Their ideas and their example continue to inform the work of thousands of counsellors, but at this moment the students are uneasy and disappointed. They have discovered that the gods are human, each with their own foibles and limitations. It is like the moment when we discover that Father Christmas does not exist, or that our parents do not know everything. Disillusion is painful. The world seems to lose some of its colour. Most of them do not want to catch my eye. Somewhere, although they may not be consciously aware of it, they probably blame me for the loss of their innocence. They are starting to realize that they are not going to find an expert who will give them a definitive picture of how it is done. It is a difficult moment for them, but it is the moment when they start on the long journey to explore how they might become a good counsellor, each in their own inimitable way.

Now we will set to work with another group who are taking their first steps on this journey. Before you read what they come up with, you might like to take part in this training session yourself. If so, imagine that you have decided to have some counselling. Close the book. Spend a few minutes writing down a list of the qualities that you would expect to find in a good counsellor. When you are ready, look at the list produced by a group of 16 students who were new to counsellor training.[2]

In Table 1 I have grouped similar characteristics. Each vote represents one mention of a quality in this group by a student. (Of course, some students noted more than one quality in a particular section that was important to them.) You may like to add your votes alongside those of the other students.

Table 1

List from Course Group of preferred counsellor characteristics	group votes	your vote
accepting, tolerant, non-judgemental, unshockable, respecting, without prejudice, awareness of cultural differences, enjoying difference	19	
reliable, trustworthy, secure, stable, strong, resilient, balanced, self-controlled, confidential	14	
empathic, understanding, sensitive, perceptive, observant	13	
friendly, compatible, warm, sympathetic, caring, encouraging, having goodwill, compassionate, gentle	11	
genuine, open, at ease with themselves, relaxed, positive role model	10	
mature, wealth of life experience, wealth of counselling experience, able to give practical help if needed, grounded, resourceful	10	
patient, calm, serene, allowing client space	7	
insightful, intuitive, seeing the 'baseline', able to make connections	5	
clear-thinking, objective, detached, dispassionate, not carrying client's baggage	4	
sharing same experience, knowing how it feels to be at rock bottom	4	
technical and theoretical competence, intelligent, deals with complexity	4	
tough, persistent, challenging, forceful, firm, direct	4	
not power-seeking, unselfish, not imposing own thoughts, not manipulative	4	
able to listen and remember	4	
energetic, highly motivated	3	
appearance: neat, minimum make-up, appropriate tone of voice	3	
good communicator	2	
spiritual awareness and care	2	
sense of humour	2	

At the beginning of their training students look at a counsellor in much the same way as a new client does at first; they are concerned with whether the counsellor's personality is warm and accepting. They are weighing up the qualities they would look for in a person in whom they would wish to confide. The items which scored ten or more usually meet with a fair measure of agreement in the group. It is as important to a client that their counsellor can accept them as it is for someone arranging a house sale to be sure that their solicitor knows the law on conveyancing. Acceptance, trustworthiness, empathy, compassion, genuineness and maturity are characteristics which are generally accepted as the stock-in-trade of the profession. It is only when enough of these elements are in place that the attention of the student or the prospective client turns to the ways in which the counsellor might deal with the information and feelings brought to them.

It is at this point that differences emerge. We came upon them first in the debate about the relative merits of Gloria's famous therapists. Now students are speaking up for their choice between characteristics which can easily seem incompatible. The discussion will be going something like this:

Student A: A counsellor must have had similar experiences to me. I could never share my feelings with someone unless I knew that they had stood where I am standing.

Student B: I don't agree. I would look for someone who is objective and professional. I want to know that they know their stuff. If a counsellor was too matey I would feel suffocated.

Student C: What about empathy? That is near the top of our list. For me empathy is about caring and being involved.

Student D: Oh, I don't agree. I know my counsellor has empathized when he remembers what I tell him and he helps me to make sense of it. I would hate it if I looked at him and his eyes were full of tears or something . . .

. . . and so on. Let us leave them to their debate. You might like to reflect on what you would say about your own preferences.

We may be able to start to understand what is happening here by focusing on empathy, a quality which is viewed as important by counsellors of every school. Empathy is defined in the *Oxford English Dictionary* as: 'The power of projecting one's personality into (and so fully comprehending) the object of contemplation.'[3]

In a dictionary written for psychoanalysts, the *OED* definition is enlarged on:

The power of projecting one's personality into (and so fully comprehending) the object of contemplation. The capacity to put oneself in another's shoes. The concept implies that one is both feeling oneself into the object and remaining aware of one's own identity as another person. The word is necessary since sympathy is only used to refer to the sharing of unpleasant experiences and does not imply that the sympathizer necessarily retains his objectivity. The capacity to empathize is an essential pre-condition of doing psychoanalytical psychotherapy.[4]

The quality of empathy defined here as essential for the therapeutic process has two aspects. The first aspect is described in the everyday dictionary. It is generally accepted that empathy is the ability to project one's personality into a person or situation and so comprehend them. When we empathize with someone we first take our own awareness and allow it to be acted on, influenced, moved by their experiences and feelings. I may weep with the citizens of a war-torn city, although I am watching them from my peaceful home town. I feel the bewilderment of a client who is struggling to cope with her depression, even though I may never have experienced severe depression. I am in touch with the anguish of someone who is trying to come to terms with sudden loss, even though I have not suffered precisely the same kind of loss.

Then there is a second process, which is perhaps used more consciously in therapeutic situations, although it is present to some extent in all interactions: Even though I am experiencing these situations alongside other people, paying attention to them, trying to see things through their eyes and feel their feelings reverberate inside me, I remain myself, not them. I am not in a bombed city. The painful depression is not, at this moment, shadowing my life. I have not been retired from work against my will. I can separate myself; observe and listen and attend to what is special and individual to the person who is talking to me and to the ways in which they experience their life, the ways perhaps in which they are different to me. If I cannot do this, I will jump to conclusions about what they 'must' be feeling; conclusions based, of course, on what *I* would feel if I were in their shoes.

There are two processes here, and most of us will 'naturally' be more aware of one than the other. Somewhere along the line – who knows whether as a result of our 'nature' or our 'nurture' – we will be more inclined to search out those who feel with us, or to feel more comfortable with someone who sits back and observes and questions what is happening. (There are a few people who do not comfortably or willingly engage with the feelings and experiences of others at all. I think we can safely say that they will not have the ability or the motivation to make good counsellors, and that if they did present themselves for counsellor training, it is unlikely that they would be selected.)

What we can see happening is our all too human tendency to focus on what is familiar and feel threatened by what is different. The 'get in there and feel group' can feel very threatened by the 'observe, reflect and explain' group, and vice versa. If these student counsellors are to become good 'empathizers', they will need to develop their ability to be what the psychotherapist Patrick Casement calls 'participant observers',[5] keeping both processes operating in parallel. This will only happen when they have gone through the painstaking work of trying out their skills in many simulated counselling sessions (role-plays) with their fellow students as guinea pig clients. As they receive honest feedback, they will start to see where their strengths and weaknesses lie.

Student taking role of client in simulated counselling session to student taking role of counsellor

'I felt you were really with me, but you seemed to be as overwhelmed by my feelings as I was. It would have been useful if, once I had got all that rage off my chest, you had helped me to look at exactly what was so overwhelming about Christmas with my in-laws.'

Feedback comment from another 'client' to her 'counsellor' after the same simulation

'It was really good that you noticed that I looked away from you every time I mentioned my in-laws. I realized just how hard I find it to look at my feelings about them. I do want to turn away from them but it was hard to tell you that. I could see that you were interested and trying to work out what was happening but I wasn't sure that you cared.'

We could examine most of the qualities named on the students' list. As we reflect on how they might be used in practice, we will discover that these seemingly simple and straightforward characteristics are all complex and multifaceted. In practice, as with empathy, we would discover that there are some aspects on which we focus and some we miss, and that our way of responding will seem to us to be the right way.

At this point I present trainees with another question. Many of the qualities on the list can be described as personality traits. If this is so, are good counsellors born or made? Can the characteristics of good counselling be learned or do they depend on having a particular kind of personality to begin with? I think that the exploration of empathy demonstrates that prospective counsellors do need to bring into training an ability to engage willingly with feelings and relationships and an interest in what makes people 'tick'. Then it is important that they can take risks and try out their skills. In the process they must be able to hear that they are in some ways insensitive and uncomprehending, without becoming too discouraged and losing the strengths that they have. The principal tool of a good counsellor is his own personality, just as the principal tool of the good athlete is her body. Both need to test their fitness out in practice, discover their strengths and weaknesses, deal with the frustration of the times when nothing goes right and work to stay as fit as possible, if they are to give of their best.

Before we leave the students' list, we should pay attention to some interesting items which have received around two or three 'votes'. These attributes will be very important to the individuals who have listed them. It will often be hard for the other students to understand why. Sometimes the requirements will be really quirky: 'I have this thing about red hair. I could not imagine trusting someone with red hair.' Sometimes they will be about shared values, a particular religious standpoint for example. They may reveal an antipathy to, or preference for, a gender, or an age group, or a social background.

These revulsions or attractions have their roots in our personal history. They often remain unconscious and powerful, influencing our perceptions of events and our style of relating, for good or ill. Their origins are often hidden in the unconscious. Sometimes they keep us fixed in patterns of response which limit or skew our lives.

I had a maths teacher when I was eight or nine who made my life a misery. She reserved a bitter stream of sarcasm and humiliation for those of us who were slow to grasp the intricacies of long division. This 'dragon' wore hairy tweed suits and sensible shoes. She had tightly permed hair and she looked at me sternly over the top of wire-rimmed half-spectacles. I escaped from her when I changed schools at 11 and I thought that I had forgotten her and consigned all those miserable encounters to a locked file marked 'bitter experience'.

When I grew up I became a primary school teacher. I never found it easy to teach maths. When I had been teaching for four years, an inspector came to the school and observed a maths lesson I was teaching. After she had gone, the head teacher called me to her study. 'Val,' she said, 'the inspector tells me that you need some help to improve your maths teaching.' She went on to explain further, but I did not hear what she was saying. I was a child again, with the dragon looking at me over her spectacles and telling me how useless I was. I did not realize at the time that this was what had happened. All I knew was that I felt inadequate and very small. 'It is all right, Val,' the head teacher said, looking at my stricken face. 'I am sure that we can sort this out.' She sat opposite me, a friendly, helpful woman, full of affection and concern, but all I saw was the dragon. It took a good deal of patient help on her part, and anguished effort from me, before I had any confidence in my ability to teach maths to five-year-olds.

The head teacher gave me a therapeutic experience, by not being the harsh critic I expected. She did not dismiss my anxieties. She was not upset when I found it hard to believe that she could assist me. She patiently helped me to find where I was stuck and to untie the knots. I owe her a lot.

The students are concerned that a counsellor should meet their needs, but even if someone matched them to a counsellor who fitted all their requirements, they would still see this relationship filtered through their past experiences. Indeed, it is important that they should, because their reactions hold the key to the issues for which they seek counselling. All counsellors have to be prepared to be on the receiving end of the kind of reaction I had to my head teacher. Technically in counselling we describe this kind of response as transference. It happens when I ascribe to a person with whom I am in relationship now, aspects of people with whom I have had significant relationships in the past, so that it feels as if things are the same now as they were back then.

A good counsellor is able to accept, as my head teacher could, that their client is seeing them in a particular way, which is not in fact how they actually are, and to respond without becoming defensive and without retaliation. That is easier said than done. Once I had a client who at the first session said, 'I really hate people who . . .' and went on to list the components of a lifestyle which described me perfectly. When I had stopped gaping like a goldfish, I set to work to try to understand her antipathies. A long time later I discovered that the roots of her reaction lay with parents who had treated the client's unconventional lifestyle with contempt and sighed over her failure to acquire one which fitted their aspirations.

It is important to be able to trust that behind all these seemingly inexplicable reactions is a life story which will reveal patterns of events and relationships that contain the clues to the client's present behaviour. The counsellor's interest in the archaeological endeavour of exploring these origins must be stronger than her need to be seen as always kind or wise or loving. This calls for a reasonable level of personal maturity and stability. Clients need to feel that they are with someone who is able to go as deep and as far into their experiences as is necessary, if they are to find healing. This may mean their counsellor being prepared to be on the receiving end of hatred, fear, contempt, fury, desire . . . pretty well any feeling you can think of.

If we are to take on this kind of work, we should also be ready and able to recognize our limitations. At one of the counselling agencies for which I worked we had links with a psychiatrist to whom we could send clients who required a psychiatric assessment. The psychiatrist was well known and acknowledged as an expert in her field. She committed suicide. Her death was the subject of reports in the local press. During the weeks that followed we had to struggle with our own sense of shock and loss and the effects of her death on clients who had known her. We had all believed that the wise doctor knew how to cope with life. Finding that, for whatever reason, she had in the end found life intolerable was a blow to our security and left several people feeling that they were lost in the jungle without a guide.

This experience taught me two things: first, that none of us is indestructible, for all of us have a breaking point. Second, that our clients depend on our ability to recognize that there may be times when we are not able to work, because we cannot take the uncertainty, the responsibility, or the sheer psychological buffeting. We may need all our emotional energy to cope with something in our own lives. At these times we should not be practising.

You will remember that the counsellor characteristics which were top priority on the students' list were: acceptance, tolerance, being non-judgemental, unshockability, respect, lack of prejudice, awareness and enjoyment of difference. Of course we all have limitations and sticking points. One of the purposes of counsellor training and the personal therapy which all counsellors should undergo is to help us discover what shocks us, disturbs us, or fills us with rage or disgust. Our tolerance should be extended by our training, but there may still be experiences which cut so deep that it is hard for us to retain any measure of objectivity about them.

I have seen counsellors struggle with the challenge to their deeply held values posed by supporting someone who chooses to make a decision which is incompatible with those values. I have worked with colleagues who have suffered through their work with someone who has a political stance which is unacceptable to them. I have seen how painful it can be to try to understand a client who was a citizen of a country which was the enemy, in a war which scarred the counsellor's life. The encounter can be difficult, but sometimes the struggle to accept and understand can be healing for counsellor and client. Conversely, if I feel that someone is easy to know, or that I can understand them because they are just like me, I can be lulled into a false sense of security. At these times I am in danger of operating on 'automatic pilot' and losing the objective dimension of empathy.

Perhaps balance is the quality which links all the others together. It is important to be able to pay attention to several dimensions concurrently; what I am feeling, what the client is feeling, what is on the surface, what is happening beneath the surface, what is happening in the present, what happened in the past . . . The list is much longer. Our clients rely on us to help them to make links and connections, to find shapes and patterns of meaning in the jumble of perceptions, feelings and experiences that they bring to us. Since every new client is, of course, unique, this endeavour is endlessly creative and challenging.

4
The Skills of a Good Counsellor

How To Be a Bad Counsellor

A psychologist called Joseph Weizenbaum designed a computer program to simulate human conversation. He programmed the computer to respond like a non-directive counsellor. Here is a snippet from a 'counselling' session between a human 'client' and 'Eliza', the computer program.[1] (The computer's words are in italics.)

'Men are all alike.'

'In what way?'

'They're always bugging us about something or other.'

'Can you think of a specific example?'

'My boyfriend made me come here.'

'Your boyfriend made you come here.'

'He says I'm depressed much of the time.'

'I am sorry to hear that you are depressed . . .'

As the 'client' tells their story, the computer responds, using a repertoire of stock replies, in response to certain triggers. If the 'client' reports a troubling emotion – fear, sadness, anger, etc. – the computer responds with 'I am sorry to hear that you are afraid, sad, etc.' as appropriate. If the client generalizes they are asked for an example.

On some occasions the 'counselling session' with the computer ran smoothly and the guinea pig 'clients' got quite attached to their 'counsellor'. Other sessions went less well. Here is a similar program, devised by K. M. Colby,[2] getting in a fix with a 'client'. (Again the computer's part is in italics.)

'We want to focus on your relations with people who bother you most.'

'That is easy, a surfeit of children in too small a space.'

'Is it?'

'Yes.'

'Can you describe an example?'

'Of what?'

'I see.'

'No, you don't . . .'

The computer fails to recognize the unusual phrase 'a surfeit of children in too small a space' and responds to the earlier part of the sentence 'that is easy', which is in its repertoire. These computer

programs behave like counsellors who have been inadequately prepared for their work. Both may convince for a time but neither will be
able to cope with more than a limited repertoire. Any departure from
the situations for which they have prepared will produce absurd
responses or repetitiveness. It is easy to find a course where you can
learn to offer a sympathetic ear and give some stock responses – in other
words, to be programmed to act like a counsellor – but if we work like
this we short-change our clients and ourselves. We become a device for
the production of clichés, and this kind of work damages the good
name of the counselling profession as well as being unproductive for
counsellor and client.

A little learning truly is a dangerous thing, particularly when you aim
to take up the responsible task of working with someone's private,
personal and secret life. I was told of a bereavement visitor who had
been to a course to develop her counselling skills. She was asked to visit
a widow. 'How long is it since your husband died?' she asked, setting
her body, no doubt, into that strange stance which is meant to indicate
attention and concern, and looks remarkably like a blackbird which has
just caught sight of a particularly juicy worm. 'Three months,' the
widow replied. 'Ah,' said her visitor, casting her mind back to the
handout she had been given by her trainer on the stages of grief. 'You
must be up to anger by now.' Unfortunately we have no record of her
hapless victim's response, but it is safe to assume that she did not find
this encounter therapeutic.

The skills of counselling can be learned and practised of course, like
the skills of teaching, or interviewing. There are modes of discourse
which are especially appropriate to each of these specialized forms of
human encounter but, just as food tastes very different when prepared
by your Aunty Flo or a great chef, it is the attitude, commitment and
creative talent of the counsellor which gives the encounter its
distinctive flavour. One does a workmanlike job with the skills she has
learned, she probably does little harm and not much good either.
Another brings all his creative energy to the job, and in so doing helps
his clients to find 'life more abundant' in all kinds of ways. Above all, he
does not seek to fit them into a preconceived picture of how they
'should' be, but helps them to enjoy living in their own unique way.

Counselling is a science and an art. Of course theory and techniques
are important, but only as a means to an end. Our knowledge must
become part of us until we can exercise what the psychotherapist
Patrick Casement (note[5] Chapter 3) calls our 'internal supervisor' to
monitor what is happening and to reflect on what it means, and how we
might best respond. This involves balancing system and spontaneity,
intimacy and objectivity and much else besides. Becoming a counsellor

is a lifelong endeavour. How can you learn how it is done without becoming like the computer program, a producer of stock responses to life's pitfalls? What are the skills of a good counsellor?

Starting from the Beginning – Paying Attention

The first skill of a good counsellor is paying attention; not just listening, as some would have you believe, although that is part of it. If you have ever sought out the help of a counsellor yourself, you will remember how sensitive you were to their response to you, how important it was to feel that they were really really wanting to get to know you, and to feel that you would be accepted, and not judged and condemned.

Of course it is important that we listen to our clients' words, but around and behind and beneath the words there is much more that needs attention, both in them and in ourselves. Sometimes my body will pick something up before it has been spoken. Sometimes I will have an overwhelming sense of a feeling, which has not been overtly expressed. Like a good detective, or researcher, the counsellor collaborates with the client to notice as much as possible; to follow clues, form hypotheses about the way the clues fit together, discard hypotheses which don't hold water, notice a fragment of a clue just visible in a corner which is of central importance after all, sit in total confusion, and so on.

Join me now as I work to get to know a new client. Read my account of this first encounter with Joan, from the telephone call to the silence. Be aware of your own reactions, as well as what is happening in the client. Make notes of your thoughts as you read. If you find it helps you to focus your thoughts, keep in mind the points listed below.

● How are you feeling, as you settle down to read her story? (Are you hungry and thinking about lunch, eager to know what happens, apprehensive . . . ?) Be aware as you read of changes in your feelings.
● What do you imagine Joan's feelings are during these encounters?
● Make a note of anything in this description which particularly takes your attention and sticks in your mind.
● List everything you know about Joan from this account. Try to make a distinction between what you *know* and what you assume or infer.
● What else do you want to know about Joan and the situation she has described? Why do you want to know it? (to fill a gap, to convince yourself that Joan is a good woman, because you are curious, etc . . .)
● Can you imagine yourself acting as Joan did? Under what circumstances?

Of course, many of the clues are more difficult to find when you read an account of this meeting on the page, rather than meeting with Joan face to face, but there should be enough information for you to begin to try out your skills in paying attention.

Joan's Story

A woman sits across from me in my consulting room. She rang a week ago. She had been given my name by a colleague who refers clients to me sometimes. 'Something has happened, which I thought I could work out on my own,' she said in that telephone conversation, 'but I think I might need some help.' She sighed. 'I am not sure if you can help me. Perhaps I just need to pull myself together.' I explained to her that she can come for an assessment, so that she and I can look together at whether coming to me for counselling might be useful to her. I gave her a session time and instructions on how to reach my consulting room and took her name and telephone number.

Joan arrives for this first session five minutes late. 'Sorry I am late,' she says. 'The journey was difficult and I had trouble finding you.' She sits across from me. She is fairly tall and slight. Her clothes are neat and businesslike. She is all neutral colours; brown hair, grey sweater, darker grey skirt, black shoes, no make-up, no perfume. I guess that she is around 35 years old. She sits on the edge of the chair, half turned away from me, looking at the patterned rug on the floor in front of her, with her feet neatly together and her hands clasped tightly in her lap. Her shoulders are raised and hunched forward, giving her a hollow-chested look. I explain again that this is an exploratory session, during which we will have the opportunity to see whether coming to me for counselling might be useful for her. 'Tell me about yourself and what brings you here,' I say.

Joan sighs, looks down at her hands, which are clasped tightly now, her knuckles white. She briefly turns her head to glance at me and then looks back down at her hands. She begins to tell her story. I pay attention, occasionally asking her to clarify something.

> I am a primary school teacher. I work mostly with 10- and 11-year-olds. I have been a teacher for 13 years, ever since I qualified. Mostly I work full-time, part-time when my children were small. I have two children; Natalie is 11 and Simon is eight. I enjoy my work. (She flashes a sudden, sharp look at me – a darting glance is the phrase that passes through my mind, then she continues.) Things are fine at home, apart from the usual odd row. Jim, my partner, works very hard. Sometimes I get fed up with that, then we have rows about him

not spending enough time with the children, that kind of thing. What happened came out of the blue . . . (She pauses.)

I'm a good teacher. (That sharp glance again.) I spend a lot of time preparing lessons. I choose to work in an inner-city school because I think that education is the only road out of a life of poverty and disillusionment for those kids. I know, I was brought up in Tower Hamlets. It was education that got me and my husband where we are today. We are not rich, but we do have a house, car, kids with new clothes, not cast-offs. I teach maths, useful knowledge, real-life stuff, not like the nonsense they get given most of the time.

(As she says this she turns in the chair to face me. Her chin is up and she has fixed an intent gaze on my face. Her fists are clenched on the arms of the chair. Then, as she falls silent, she subsides and turns aside into her earlier position, with a heavy sigh. Silence falls. After perhaps a minute she begins to speak again. This time her voice is low and hesitant.)

I shouldn't have hit her. I don't know what made me do it. One minute I was helping a group of Year Fives with some work I had set them, the next moment all hell broke loose. (A long pause.) I've had trouble with Marilyn before, mind you. She seems to know just how to wind me up, but I'm used to her. This time something happened inside me. It was when little Samantha said, 'Miss, she's taken my calculator.' I just saw red. I know Samantha's mother works nights in the factory to pay for her school things. Marilyn denied it of course, but I knew by her face she had done it and not for the first time . . . Then I hit her hard across the head with Samantha's ruler.

(There is a silence. Joan sighes heavily several times. She looks as though she is about to cry but her jaw is set firmly. Her hands are clenched tightly together.)

Go through this encounter and write what you noticed about yourself and Joan. When you have completed your notes read mine and compare them with yours. Notice the differences and similarities in the way I pay attention and the way you pay attention.

My Notes on Attending to Joan

The Telephone Call

The telephone is ringing. It is the end of a busy working day, and I am tired. All I want to do is put my feet up. I pick up the phone. The woman at the end of the line says, 'I was given your name by X.' (X is someone who sometimes refers people to me for counselling, so I know that I am speaking to a prospective client.) I need a new client to replace the space in my practice left by a client who finished counselling last week. In other words, I am feeling ambivalent about this call. My mind was winding down and now has to go into reverse and concentrate.

I focus attention on Joan, setting on one side for the moment my own preoccupations as much as I can. I listen to my voice as I speak, for signs of impatience or tiredness. As I listen to Joan I realize that she too is ambivalent – 'I thought I could work it out on my own . . .' 'I think I might need some help . . .' 'I am not sure if you can help me . . .' 'Perhaps I just need to pull myself together.' What do I know about her? Only that she is wrestling with two dilemmas; one is the as yet nameless problem, and the other is whether or not she wants to come for counselling. Do I need to know more? Not at this point, only practical details of her name and telephone number in case I need to contact her again.

Without being very consciously aware of it, I have made some judgements about Joan being, at least potentially, someone who could benefit from counselling. I offer her an assessment session. This acknowledges that neither of us is yet ready to commit ourselves to her coming for counselling. It establishes that ambivalence is an appropriate feeling to have at this point, and it offers her the chance to come and struggle with it with me. I am not making any reassuring noises. I am not promising to help, but I am offering her a clear reliable space in which to pay attention to her unclear situation. Anything else would feel misleading, because it would be based on unwarranted assumptions, although to reassure Joan and myself I would like to be able to say, 'Of course counselling will help', 'I am sure we will be able to sort out your problem', and so on. Each of us has to live with uncertainty at this point and that always evokes some measure of anxiety.

It is the start of the time set for Joan's first session. I am sitting in my consulting room, but she has not yet arrived. I call the telephone conversation to mind and muse on why she is not yet here. Has she turned her back on the idea of counselling? Is indecisiveness part of her difficulty and she is demonstrating this difficulty through her behaviour (technically known as acting out)? Is she giving me another message by her actions; for example that she wants to come, but finds this difficult? These are all hypotheses at the moment, but I will pay special attention to how she deals with her lateness when she arrives . . . if she arrives . . . The doorbell rings.

The Arrival

'Sorry I am late . . . The journey was difficult and I had trouble finding you.' I hear this as both a factual statement and a symbolic statement about Joan's state of mind and her feelings in relation to counselling. My hypothesis about her state of mind now is that she wants to do this and do it properly, but that she experiences two difficulties; whether she can manage the journey to and through counselling and whether we will be able to make contact, physically and emotionally. These are speculations at the moment, of course. I must be prepared to rethink them in the light of new evidence. For now it is enough that she has got here, but not without difficulty.

Start of the First Session

Joan starts to tell me what has brought her. Sitting with her for the first time I am aware of her tension and of her neutral appearance. As I look at Joan hunched forward in her chair, I realize that my shoulders too have tightened. I feel vaguely apprehensive, but I am not sure why. I note that it may be because Joan does not look at me. It is always disconcerting when someone will not meet our gaze. She is hidden away. All the hard and bony parts of her body are curved around the vulnerable parts. Here is a clue that could signify many things. She is hidden ('defended' in psychological jargon). From what is she hiding?

I feel a mixture of anticipation and anxiety; what is the 'something' which has happened to Joan? Will I be able to do some useful work with her? Will she stick it out when the going gets rough? Will both of us get through it without unbearable trauma? I register these feelings and concentrate on Joan as she starts to tell me about herself. The first pieces of information she gives me are about her work and her family. To be more specific, they are about her involvement with children, as a teacher and as a mother. Why might she have started with this? I store that question away in the growing file of unanswered questions.

Her partner comes into the picture. 'Things are fine but he neglects the children.' Does she mean their actual children, Natalie and Simon? Or that the child aspect of her is feeling neglected? Or that he doesn't pay enough attention to 'child' pursuits; playing, relaxing, seeing things afresh, etc.? Or a mix of all these things?

Then she fixes her gaze on me and talks about her passion for her work; her 'mission' I want to call it. I feel held by her scrutiny. I see behind it the defiant determination of all the innumerable children who have fought their way out of poverty and deprivation to a better life. For a second I wonder what will happen if she feels that *I* am impeding her progress. I feel what I imagine to be an intense will to overcome in Joan, to fight anything that gets in her way.

The Moment of Truth

Then she tells me the terrible truth. Ah, so that is it. That is the trigger for all these feelings. I feel the horror of it with her. Her self-esteem has taken a hard knock. It is as if she has spent her lifetime building a strong, reliable, and efficient house to provide her with living space and shelter, only to have a raging animal come up from the basement and undo a large piece of her hard work. Where has this come from? Why did it break out now? What fuels this rage? This will be at the heart of the work we might do together. In the silence I sit and hold in my mind the scene in that classroom. I focus attention on Joan. I am aware that she is holding herself tightly together in the face of all this. From behind this control her feelings break through with great intensity. The dominant sense is of sadness and anger. How can I pay attention to her at this point in a way that will most help her to live with, to come to understand, and to deal with this situation? Can I acknowledge my own capacity for violence and use my awareness to empathize with the feelings which led Joan to this violent act? Can I work with the intensity of her feelings, even when I am on the receiving end of them, without becoming overwhelmed?

Comparing Notes

Each of us has a particular way of perceiving situations and people, which depends on our own past experience. Our perception is inevitably biased and distorted. Some things set off echoes in our memory and make a powerful impact, some have not featured significantly in our own lives and so they fade into the background. It is said that when Captain Cook's ships sailed close to what became known as Cook Island, the islanders did not 'see' the ships. They had never seen large sailing ships before and had no means of perceiving them. It is useful to share our perceptions of a situation with someone else. They will often 'see' aspects of it which are not so clear to us, or even completely absent from our own perception.

Joan has been violently angry with a child. If you were here with me now we could usefully reflect on our own experience of violence between adults and children. If we could compare notes there is probably a good deal we could learn from each other. I need to know the way I perceive, otherwise my attention will be distorted by what I expect to see. We do not yet know what Joan perceives to be the main difficulty in this situation and, because we do not like to be in the dark, we fill the gaps from our own store of experience. For example, if I fear that the darker sides of my personality may be revealed, and that the revelation will expose me to shame and condemnation, I am likely to see that as Joan's main problem too. If I have led a sheltered life I may find it difficult to cope with feelings being expressed in such a direct way.

Whilst I am paying attention to my own perceptions I must pay attention to Joan's perceptions too, and all the time ask myself, 'How does she experience and understand these events?' I may discover that Joan is 'sure' that I must be condemning her for what she has done. She may feel that I 'must' have had a comfortable childhood and could not possibly understand how it feels to be deprived. From such powerful perceptions I will be able to gradually understand the way Joan makes sense of what is happening and how her interpretation of events affects the ways that she understands and deals with them.

Finding the Right Words

Once we have attended as fully as possible to the encounter with a client the next step is to respond to what is happening. A new counsellor sat down with her first client. 'I am really nervous,' the client said. 'But I expect you're used to this. Have you done a lot of counselling?' The new counsellor's reply is not recorded, but she had to be fast on her feet to respond usefully. What would you have said? So far in the session with Joan, my responses have been simple. I have explained how to get to the first session. I have invited her to tell me about herself and what brings her to counselling. I have asked her to clarify any statements I do not understand. I am wanting to give her a clear space in which to talk, to let her know that I am interested and paying attention. I am trying not to interfere with her train of thought. Let us go back now to where we left her. She has just said, 'Then I hit her hard across the head with Samantha's ruler.' There is a silence. Joan sighs heavily several times. She looks as though she is about to cry but her jaw is set firmly. Her hands are clenched tightly together.

Clearly this moment calls for special sensitivity. My response could be therapeutic, or destructive, or just not particularly useful. What would you say? I cannot give you a right answer, much as I might wish that I could. What I can do is invite you to look with me at some things to be considered in choosing how to respond.

Why Respond?

The short answer is: in order to progress the counselling work. The longer answer is to help our clients find more fulfilling ways to experience their lives and to enable them to free themselves from habitual, stereotyped and inhibiting reactions. Counselling responses are more careful, more purposive than everyday conversational responses. Before we return to look for a response to Joan it would be useful to reflect on some therapeutic styles of responding.

Moving from Reacting to Responding

In conversation with a friend I usually reply to their statements without much thought. If Joan was a friend I might sympathize with her; tell her about times my temper got the better of me; take her side; generally express solidarity; but that is not what Joan is paying me for. With a friend I would react. To respond I need to process my own feelings and use them to inform me about what is happening with Joan. Then I need to pay attention to how she is different from me, so that I do not assume that she will respond in the same way. Several times, in my account of my time with her, I did this.

- At the time of the telephone call I registered that we were both ambivalent and monitored whether my tiredness was affecting my voice.
- When she is late I muse on possible reasons.
- At the start of the session I register tension in us both.

You will be able to find other examples in the account. It is worth giving some thought to the difference between reacting and responding. How might you react and respond to the following statements?

- She's a selfish manipulative bitch. All women are the same.
- Other people have terrible childhoods, I know, but mine was totally wonderful. My parents were just perfect.
- It's all right for you. I expect you have plenty of money, children who behave well all the time, etc. You don't know what it's like to be depressed/poor/confused, etc.
- I have been coming to see you for six weeks now and I don't feel any better. In fact, if anything I feel worse. I have told you what is wrong. If you were any good you would tell me how to sort this mess out.

Statements like this can evoke a powerful reaction. It takes practice and self-discipline not to retaliate and defend oneself, but to choose a response which will be therapeutic for the client.

Ways of Responding

Here are some possible modes of response. I am sure that you could add to the list.

Bearing witness to remembered key experiences: This is happening already with Joan. If I can show her that I have heard what she has shared, and that I empathize with her experience, she no longer has to carry it alone. One way of doing this is by finding a way to summarize the situation, as she has described it and her feelings about it, and so reflect them back to her, so that she can take a closer look. (You can find wonderful examples of this kind of response in a book called *Dibs*.[3])

Making connections: As individuals, and in our relationships, we tend to perpetuate ways of dealing with things, without knowing why. (Freud called this 'repetition compulsion'.[4]) A counsellor can draw attention to repeated patterns, invite her client to explore their history and help them to examine whether this pattern of response still serves the client well. I may, for example, point out to someone that, whenever she talks about mothers and their babies, she stresses the sacrifice made by the mother to care for her child and the thoughtlessness with which the child accepts her care, and then wonder with her why this might be. Has she experienced this pattern in her dealings with *all* mothers and their babies or with one or two significant ones? Did her mother constantly emphasize how much she had given up for her baby? Is it always like that for mothers and babies? She may be put off the idea of being a mother herself by this image of unrewarding drudgery.

Joan believes that, to escape from deprivation, you have to fight, to concentrate on 'useful' subjects and not to let anyone get in your way. It may well be useful for her to reflect on how she acquired these convictions and whether following them is always useful in her present life. I am sure that you could think of other examples from your own experience. The clue to the presence of these patterns is frequent use of the words 'always' and 'never' as in: 'People always let me down', 'I never succeed in what I set out to do.'

Looking at possibilities: There was a client who was trying to make a decision. For weeks he looked at what he might do. The impasse became more and more painful. To help things along, I suggested that we examine all the options he had looked at so far. I listed them. (It would probably have been better to get him to list them.) 'Ah,' he said, with a look of relief. 'You think I ought to do . . .' He named the first option in the list. I struggled on. 'No,' I said. 'I was listing them all so that you could see them alongside each other.' With a happy, conspiratorial grin he said, 'But you always put the best option first and then you rush through the rest.' All I could do was admit that he had 'sussed me out' and thank him for drawing my unconscious manipulation to my attention. In the event, he was so pleased with himself to have been one step ahead of me, it spurred him on to make an independent decision. He had some reason for feeling that he would make a better job of it than me.

Silence: If you pay close attention to silences, you will discover that they can take many forms. Some are like pregnancies; something is growing and if you wait it will be born when its time comes. Some silences are like a wilderness and the person lost in them may need to be assured that you are there with them. Sometimes you can feel someone hiding in the silence from an aspect of their experience they are afraid to meet, or are afraid of you meeting. Then it can help for you to stay in touch with their fear and their longing to come out of hiding.

If we go back to where we left Joan, she has just said, 'Then I hit her hard across the head with Samantha's ruler.' There is a silence, in which she sighs heavily several times. She looks as if she is about to cry but her jaw is set. Her hands are clenched tightly together. What might be going on in this silence? How would you respond to her? Here are the possibilities I listed. (The list is not exhaustive and you may think of something better.)

- Bearing witness to remembered key experiences
- Making connections
- Looking at possibilities
- Silence

Once again, there is no right answer. What often happens, if I do this kind of exercise with a group of trainee counsellors, is that at this point some of them will become frustrated with me. 'But what is Joan going to *do*?' they say and they offer possible solutions to her plight. They hope that I have a solution up my sleeve, but of course I do not. (Perhaps you have been experiencing some of these feelings yourself.) The frustration experienced here is ultimately with the uncertainty of life itself. There are no answers. Perhaps one of the most useful ways to respond to Joan at this point is to empathize with her struggle to deal with the profound uncertainty of her situation. Sheldon Kopp, an American psychotherapist, describes this situation in his book, *If You Meet the Buddha on the Road, Kill Him.*[5] He says:

> It is as if I stand in the door of my office, waiting. The patient enters and makes a lunge at me, a desperate attempt to pull me into the fantasy of taking care of him. I step aside. The patient falls to the floor, disappointed and bewildered. Now he has a chance to get up and try something new ... The seeker comes in hope of finding something definite, something permanent, something unchanging upon which to depend. He is offered instead the reflection that life is just what it seems to be, a changing, ambiguous, ephemeral mixed bag. It may often be discouraging, but it is ultimately worth it, because that is all there is.

There are no clear, unambiguous answers to life's difficulties. Joan, along with many other people who seek counselling, may hope that there are. Many counsellors take up counselling because they want to find answers too. All of us have to face our disappointment when this is not possible. So what, apart from listening and sensitive responding, do I offer to Joan and to all my clients?

A Safe Space

When was the last time that someone gave you their undivided attention for 50 minutes? Concentrated caring attention is a rare and precious commodity. A counsellor provides this, in a setting which is designed to be a safe place for exploration. Here are some of the factors which help to make this possible:

- day, time and length of session clear, consistent and known beforehand
- counselling room which is private, comfortable, not too plush or too much of a shambles
- confidentiality assured
- counsellor trained, reliable, skilled
- counsellor not part of client's family or circle of friends
- counsellor takes responsibility for managing all of this

Could you provide this consistently over time? It would mean not taking long breaks or moving your consulting room around too much, being reasonably healthy and committed to the work. It could be useful to reflect on whether this is the way you would want to work.

Playing a Part in the Drama

If you have ever had the care of a teenager you will know that they have a tendency at times to see people as if they have one dimension. They regard them as heroes, or villains, or fools, or founts of wisdom, beautiful, or ugly beyond belief. In the process they are establishing their own identity through sifting, incorporating, rejecting, fighting and adoring what they see to be the attributes of those around them. In adolescence this process is particularly active. As clients we go through a similar process; we may need a counsellor to carry the role of 'the father who will not let me do what I want', or 'the mother who seems to offer much but who, like the witch in Hansel and Gretel, will trap me if I take her gifts', or 'the lover who will take me in her arms so that I need never feel alone again'. The potential roles are endless.

Joan may see me as someone she has to fight to get what she needs.

She may feel that I cannot possibly know what it means to struggle as she has struggled. She may think that I am only in it for the money, that I would never hit out in anger . . . There are many possibilities. I will need to be able to accept these perceptions while she looks at them, and that may mean being told that I am useless, mercenary, smug, middle-class, unfeeling, cold and any number of other uncomfortable things. Of course, she may also see me as wonderful, all-knowing, capable, infinitely patient, unmaterialistic, etc. These idealizations can be seductive and then I may be tempted to encourage them. It can be very hard to hold on to who I am and not to retaliate in this situation, but it is important for both of us that I try.

The counsellor needs to be able to accept that this is how the client sees her but not to take on the role. The skills needed to deal with this situation are complex but if a counsellor can get it right, that can be a great help in shifting the 'always' and 'never' fixed patterns I talked about in the last section. If I believe that 'people always let me down' and I see a counsellor for any length of time, I will become anxious that she too will let me down, because it is 'always' so. If instead, the counsellor can allow herself to feel the strength of my anxiety *and* not let me down, but remain reliable, the conditions are in place for me to look afresh at this unconscious fixed pattern, and to ask myself whether it does have *always* to be the same.

Change and Insight

As we have seen, there are no easy answers to be found, but it is possible to come to a new understanding of what is happening, and that can make all the difference. Each discovery I make changes my picture of who I am, sometimes in a small way, sometimes considerably. This can be disconcerting, exciting, sometimes shocking.

Awareness and insight are two of the main goals of therapeutic work. When I become more aware of how I deal with life, and understand more about why I deal with life in the way that I do, I am more able to make meaning out of what is happening to me. When I understand more about why I am as I am, I become free to choose how I respond. I gain freedom and maturity, but there is a price to pay. If I am free to choose how to respond, I have to take responsibility for my responses. It is then harder to bury my head in the sand when I do not like what I see, or to disclaim responsibility for my decisions and actions. I gain freedom and autonomy and lose illusions. The difficulty is that some illusions are very comforting and their loss can feel traumatic. Once the illusion is lost it cannot easily be put back in place.

A man was leading a double life. To those who knew him in his 'legitimate' existence he was unselfish, reliable, virtuous, conventional, hard-working. In his 'alternative' life he was hedonistic, sexy, unconventional, impulsive. His illusion was that he could lead two separate existences without harm to anyone. 'What they don't know can't hurt them.' There was one vital factor of which he was unaware: that the person he was deceiving and hurting most was himself. His 'conventional' side was insipid and lifeless, drained of the energy he was using to suppress his sexuality; and his 'wild' side was sterile, always pursuing novelty and never properly consummated because his capacity for devotion and fidelity was in the other camp.

When, with the help of a counsellor, he saw that he was hurting himself and selling short those who cared for him, he became depressed and disorientated. He embarked on a new relationship to distract him, but discovered that he could no longer 'lose himself' in it, as he had before. He blamed his counsellor for his depression. It was only when he felt that things could not be worse that he began, reluctantly, to bring his two worlds closer together. It was a long time before he found this satisfying. He described himself as 'sadder and wiser'.

In Ibsen's play *A Doll's House*,[6] Torvald Helmer, a successful lawyer, has a young wife, Nora, who he adores and cossets. He calls her his 'squirrel', his 'skylark', his 'little squanderbird' who spends his money on pretty things. She is flirty, childlike and seemingly featherbrained. In the last act of the play there is an incident which reveals Nora as a strong and resourceful woman, who once saved her husband's life by acting in a way which was ingenious but dishonest. Torvald is appalled by this revelation but says that he will forgive and protect her; that she will become his child, his 'poor helpless bewildered creature'. At this point Nora gains new insight into her marriage. She realizes that she and Torvald each have had an illusory picture of the other. She says to her husband, 'You arranged everything the way you wanted it, so that I simply took over your taste in everything – or pretended I did . . . I performed tricks for you and you gave me food and drink . . . I've been your doll-wife.'[7]

I will not reveal the extraordinary denouement which follows, but this moment of insight changes the 'doll's house' and its inhabitants irrevocably.

Here, in brief, are some common illusions:

- someday my prince will come and I will live happily ever after
- that anyone is all good, or all evil, or that the innocent and guilty parties in a situation can be readily identified
- it could never happen to me

- if I care for him/her in the right way he/she will change and love me in the way I want
- I might need to have a drink or a cigarette before I can get out of bed, but I can control my drinking/smoking

Sometimes a sudden disillusionment is the trigger that makes someone seek counselling. This may be true of Joan. She saw herself as capable and in control and then she 'snapped'. Let us return to her as she faces this.

We have been sitting in silence.

I say, 'This has been a heavy blow for you.'

Joan looks at me and her eyes fill with tears. 'I am afraid of what I might do next,' she says.

> I seem to be so angry all the time. What is the point of it all? You work hard and then get in a state over a silly mixed-up little girl. Why does she have to spoil everything? She should get on with it, work like Samantha works, like I had to work. She's just throwing away her chances and spoiling things for the others too. My mother was on her own with us and she worked so hard so that we could stay at school. We just had to get on with things, look after ourselves. I don't want my kids, any kids to go through that. I'm afraid of losing my job, of losing everything I've worked so hard for . . .

Joan stops and sighs. 'I don't know if counselling will help, but I don't know what else to do. I have always been able to sort things out for myself before, but I don't know how to sort this out.'

Joan has coped with so much on her own. I imagine that it must have been hard for her to accept that she needs help now. She may hope that I will help her to get things back under control, but her sense of control was illusory and only maintained by her being constantly on guard against any spontaneous expression of feeling, by always 'going it alone' and never allowing herself to get in touch with her loneliness and vulnerability. This incident broke through her carefully constructed defences and suddenly brought her face-to-face with the feelings behind them.

Counselling and counsellor training are disillusioning. If you go down this road you will need to be prepared to face some uncomfortable truths about yourself and to face the shock experienced by your clients when they discover that they have spent years pursuing illusory goals. Before I was a counsellor I imagined that people would be grateful if I helped them to reach a better understanding of themselves. Sometimes they are, it is true, but sometimes they would like me to 'put the genie back in the bottle' and of course that is not possible.

I always enjoy the famous scene at the end of the film *The Wizard of Oz*.[8] Four friends have 'followed the yellow brick road' to find the wizard. Each of them travels in the hope that the wizard will give them something that they think they lack. The tin man wants a heart, the lion wants courage, Dorothy wants to find her heart's desire, and the scarecrow wants a brain. They reach the wizard's palace and sure enough, there he is, an enormous figure, roaring and flashing and generally looking impressive and superhuman. Then Dorothy wanders round behind him and discovers an untidy old man, pressing buttons and pulling levers ... the wizard is a sham. The four are angry and disillusioned and afraid. How would they now find their heart's desire? Eventually they each discover that they did not need a wizard's resources, they already had their own. All they needed was the courage to go on that journey of discovery and to follow the road to the end. As they travelled along, facing dangers and caring for each other, they discovered and exercised their resources and were transformed in the process. Then came the time to part; to take their newly discovered treasures back home.

Ending

Finally, after all this investment of time and interest and concern, the counselling will come to an end. One of my clients was quite clear that one of the most important things about me was that I was expendable. She needed her partner, her other relations, her friends. She did not want to do anything that might lead to rifts with them. She could try things out with me because I was not part of her personal circle. Others find it hard to face that it is the end; they say, 'Perhaps I don't need two more sessions after all', or 'We may meet again someday.' Others bring a whole new issue to the last session. Some are relieved that they have come to the end of a painful search.

We seldom know what happens in the next chapter of the client's story. Even in a role-play exercise this can feel uncomfortable. I once called 'time' in such an exercise and a student said, 'But we can't stop now, she's halfway up a ladder.' Almost everyone who seeks counselling comes with a loss, sometimes many losses, with which they are trying to come to terms. We left Joan facing the loss of her sense of control and self-sufficiency. If she continues in counselling it is likely that she will come face-to-face with other losses. She lost the chance to have a carefree childhood. Perhaps that is one reason why she is so angry with Marilyn, who does not behave responsibly. She was deprived of her mother's attention, but her mother could do no more, so it would have been hard for Joan to say that she needed more from her. She lost the opportunity to make demands and to be angry if they were not met. (Of course there were many resources available to her too and she made good use of them. The picture is by no means all doom and gloom.)

Perhaps Joan will be able to use counselling to express her anger safely and allow herself more care and attention. We do not know the end of the story.

I can say, from my own experience, that whether I have spoken for ten minutes to someone who has called a telephone helpline, and then referred them to someone else for counselling, or worked with a client for several years, I am always left with an experience of the raw edges of loss and sometimes this triggers off memories of old painful partings in my life. If I am to be able to deal with this it is important that I have my own sources of support and satisfaction; a chance to pursue my own journey of exploration and discovery.

The end of each session is a rehearsal of the final end of counselling. Let us finish with the end of Joan's first counselling session. She has just said, 'I don't know if counselling will help, but I don't know what else to do. I have always been able to sort things out for myself before, but I don't know how to sort this out.'

(My words are in italics.)

'*What would you want to get from coming for counselling?*'

'I want to understand what is happening to me. It is all so confusing. I want to be able to control my temper so that I don't lose my job. I haven't told anyone that I'm coming. I'm afraid of what they might think.'

'*You are not sure how other people might view this. I wonder if you are also saying that you are anxious about what this might mean for you.*'

'Well yes, I always thought that counselling was something other people did; people who can't sort things out for themselves.'

'*Feeling that you can do things on your own is very important for you.*'

'Yes, I don't want anyone to tell me what to do, but counselling isn't like that, is it? It's been a relief to talk. People keep trying to give me advice, but you haven't done that. I'm still not sure whether it will solve anything, but I can let off steam here. Perhaps that will stop me blowing my top at work. I can think here, and have some time for myself. That feels good.'

'*We are coming to the end of our time, Joan. You are telling me that some things have felt good but you still have some questions about what counselling might mean for you. I'll see you this time next week and we can pick it up from there.*' (We will have one more session before we each decide whether to commit ourselves to Joan's counselling. This allows us both some thinking time before we make a decision.)

5
Knowing Yourself

I once went to a workshop for counsellors and psychotherapists on attitudes to sexuality. Halfway through the first day, the workshop leader said, 'Who knows more about sexual attitudes than a prostitute? We have invited a working prostitute here today, to talk to you about her work. In fact she has been taking part in the workshop this morning with the rest of you.' The effect of this statement was electrifying. I am certain that we all became curious about each woman in the room. I imagine many in the group responded as I did, by looking intently and covertly (not an easy thing to do) at each woman and trying to work out which of them was about to stand up and walk forward to the podium. I had just settled on a tall, elegant blonde woman, who wore very red lipstick, when, at the other side of the room, another woman rose from her seat and slowly walked to the front. She was of medium height and slight. She wore a rather severe, dark grey suit. Her hair was drawn back into a bun and she was not wearing make-up. I would have expected her to be a banker perhaps, or a civil servant. She had some very interesting observations to make about her work, including the statement that she saw her services as therapeutic.

Of course, what I was doing was looking for a match for my stereotyped image of how a prostitute looks and behaves. Some of my confusion may have arisen from her not being in her 'working clothes', but I would never have guessed how Vanessa (not her real name, of course, but a working alias she assumed for the occasion) made her living. This little episode was designed to confront us with our attitudes to the sex industry and those who work in it. Vanessa also challenged us to look at ourselves, and our attitudes to sexuality. She was particularly critical of the shallow politeness of some 'respectable' middle-class relationships.

I tell this story because it illustrates the kind of experience that I have often had in my years of working in counselling; the experience of something happening which challenges my picture of myself, of other people, of my sense of the meaning of events. Of course this can happen to anyone, in any walk of life, but being a successful counsellor involves keeping an open mind, living with uncertainty, always being prepared to discover that things are not what they seem. My aim in this chapter is to provide you with some opportunities for this kind of exploration. I suggest that you read up to the heading 'The Time of your Life' and then browse, trying things out which catch your eye. I have tried to give you a map of some of the fascinating landscape of your personality, so that you can choose which areas to visit and get to know better.

Knowing You, Knowing Me

Every time a new client sits down to embark on their first session with me I know that they are closely scrutinizing me and my consulting room, searching for clues to help them to decide whether working with me is likely to fulfil their hopes and expectations. They need assurance on some crucial questions:

- Do I care about what is happening to them?
- Can I be trusted to respect their secrets?
- Am I strong enough to deal with the frightening struggles they may have to endure?
- Will I be reliable and stick with them for as long as it takes?
- Will I disapprove of their lifestyle, beliefs, relationships . . . ?
- Am I open and genuine, or might I deceive or manipulate them?
- Might I want to have power over them and tell them how to run their lives?

I am sure this represents a fraction of the concerns of clients, as they take the enormous step of choosing a counsellor to be a companion and guide on their journey of discovery.

Vanessa challenged us to look at what constitutes a therapist, at our motivation for wanting to do this work, and she questioned our understanding of what makes a fulfilling relationship. Each client brings me face-to-face with aspects of myself which I have not previously encountered. Each challenges my preconceptions. I can only accompany them as far as I have gone myself. If I do not know how it feels to face my own uncertainties and hurts, my ability to empathize with clients will be severely limited. If I am out of touch with my feelings, or keep some of them locked in a closet, because I am ashamed of them, I will be limited in my ability to accompany someone else, as they experience the depths of their fear, or their need to be liked, or their shame about their past, or whatever it is they find it difficult to reveal. If I am fortunate and the client is courageous, they will point out my shortcomings, but sadly I may never know about the clients who make their excuses and leave counselling, because they are not able to voice their misgivings about me and about counselling.

Counselling provides a space where a client can think the unthinkable and say the unsayable. If you are to help someone to do this you must first be prepared to bring out into the open some aspects of yourself which you may well have hoped would never see the light of day. In my own training I soon discovered that, behind my urge to please, hid a mean, bitchy aspect of my personality, who I liked to indulge in secret. I would keep the smile firmly in place and snigger with 'the bitch' about the nasty thoughts only 'we' knew. It was a nasty shock the first time someone said that they had noticed her, but it gave me the opportunity to discover that I needed to sneer in secret because I was anxious about the effects of making critical, or even challenging comments out in the open. Once I discovered that I could be challenging, and still be accepted, I did not need to snigger in the corner like a naughty schoolgirl. Then I could employ freely the more useful aspects of my hidden critical eye, in ways which are more likely to be creative.

You might find it useful to join me now for a small step in your own journey of self-discovery. Remember as you set off, that whatever you find has creative potential. The more I can accept myself, the freer I am to make choices. Hiding aspects of myself away, because I fear their unacceptability, takes emotional energy which I cannot then use for living. That fixed smile I used to keep in place hurt more of me than my jaw.

Ways of Seeing

Counsellors need to be detectives, keenly observing and interpreting the evidence which is before them, and archaeologists, examining the relics of past experience, which we call memories, for the clues they contain about the time when the events which they commemorate were new. Each school of counselling favours different methods for unearthing these precious fragments and fitting them together into a meaningful picture. Each has a different explanation for how we develop and change. Perhaps that is not surprising, when we see the wealth of material waiting to be explored.

Each of us is born into a particular *time, place and culture*; we live with a group of people who constitute our *family* (using the word in its widest sense, to mean those people with whom we live and who care for us). We inherit a particular *genetic make-up* and a *family history*. From the moment of conception, *events* occur which shape our lives. We may have anxious or sick parents. We may or may not have been 'planned' and wanted. As our *body* develops we begin to experience the world outside us through our *senses*, and our inner world through our *sensations*. Once we are through birth, all of this inheritance shapes our *relationships* and *experiences*. We and those who care for us deal with events in particular ways and each have our own ways of understanding their meaning and importance. Our *memories* of what has happened to us, how it felt and how we understood it, lead us to develop *expectations* of what might happen in the future: 'That particular noise comes before a meal', 'When mother's voice sounds like that she handles me roughly.'

Gradually we acquire a set of *'rules' for living*, based on our family's values and ways of managing life: 'Big boys don't cry', 'Nobody loves clever girls.' The consequences of putting these strategies into practice feed back into our memory, and either reinforce the strategies or produce doubts about their effectiveness. My sense of myself and the way I understand experience is shaped by all these aspects of existence. The meaning I make of events contains strands from them all. My *motivation* is based on my expectation of what is satisfying and what is better avoided. The picture is complex, and beneath all the strands already mentioned run the deep currents of *the unconscious*. These undercurrents come to the surface in dreams, slips of the tongue, thoughts and feelings and actions which appear 'out of nowhere' and operate according to laws of their own, outside our conscious control. The immensity of this whole 'inscape' is awesome, and so may be experienced as intriguing and fascinating, or terrible and frightening.

> Oh the mind, mind has mountains: cliffs of fall
> Frightful, sheer, no-man-fathomed. Hold them cheap
> May who ne-er hung there.[1]

At this point perhaps the most useful thing to do is to open this treasure chest of human experience and to begin to explore a few patterns to be found in your own history. (How do you feel about this prospect? I would suggest that it is useful for intending counsellors to feel a mixture of interest and caution at this stage, if you are to treat this investigation with proper care and respect.) As you explore, notice when you are on familiar territory, when the picture is confused or vague and when you feel uncomfortable and want to change the subject.

A word of warning: If you know that there are very traumatic areas of your past, which have left you with painful unhealed scars, it is wiser to explore them with someone, possibly a counsellor, to guide and support you.

The Time of Your Life

The time and culture in which I am born and live out my life provide a context which both nurtures and circumscribes my existence and my possibilities for physical, emotional, intellectual and social development. Sigmund Freud was born in 1856 in Freiberg, a little town 150 miles north-east of Vienna, to a Jewish family. He trained as a doctor and pursued research in neurology. His progress in Vienna in this career was curtailed by anti-Semitism. If this had not been the case, would he have 'gone out on a limb' and created a new field of research, later known as psychoanalysis? We shall never know, of course. What we can find, by looking at his work, are the marks of his time and culture.

Freud grew to manhood in Vienna in the 1870s. It was a time and a place in which there was great optimism about the ability of scientific investigation to find answers to the great mysteries of life. Freud saw himself as a scientist. (It has been said that he was a poet who was trying to be a scientist.) He set himself the enormous task of establishing scientific explanations of the structure of the personality, the development of the personality, the relationship of the unconscious to consciousness, the basis of neurotic disturbances and methods for the treatment of neuroses. This grand venture bears the hallmark of an age of scientific optimism. Freud's work was driven by another aspect of his culture; in that time and place anti-Semitism was rife. Freud began his career as a brilliant and ambitious research neurologist, but his prospects in his chosen profession were curtailed by the prejudices which the medical profession of that time shared with the rest of the Viennese establishment. A less determined man might have been demoralized by this setback, but it was used by Freud as a springboard to enter uncharted territory, where there was no established hierarchy.

Take some time now to reflect on the culture into which you were born and the culture within which you have lived.

- Think about the events and the ruling Zeitgeist of the time of your life: are you a child of the 'swinging sixties' or a wartime baby? Have you lived in peace and stable prosperity or in national insecurity and social deprivation? If the prevailing climate suits us we may continue to live by it even when the cultural wind has changed, just as there are people who still sport an 'Elvis' hairstyle or bell-bottom trousers. If we dislike it, we may continue to rebel and fight against it even when the threat has passed.
- How has cultural context affected the course of your life? Where has it served to sustain, confuse or constrain you? Do you want to change any of these patterns?
- When you have thought about your time and culture you may like to note any discoveries or points for further reflection. I have known individuals who have re-found a cultural inheritance which they had earlier rejected and, in doing so, become the heirs to great riches.

A Twig on the Family Tree

Each new baby born into a family becomes the focus of the family's hopes and expectations. I once heard of someone who had an ancestor, born four generations before him, who had achieved historical notoriety as a coward. He had refused to lead his men into battle, perhaps, or lied, when to tell the truth would have been risky but right. All the male members of this family were under pressure to prove themselves in some brave endeavour. Each of them was presented, without it ever being said, with the task of doing his bit to ameliorate the 'family curse' of cowardice.

Sometimes a major clue to these hopes and expectations is to be found in your name, and the stories told in your family about the way in which it was chosen. I remember a conversation in a maternity ward between several women who had just given birth. One of them had a book of 'names and their meanings' and the discussion went something like this:

'Jeremy, that's a nice name, sounds like someone smart and gentle.'

'Yes, but what if he grows up to be a rugby player or a wrestler? Can't imagine a wrestler called Jeremy.'

'I like George, but it seems like a grown-up name somehow. It would feel strange calling a baby George.'

'My mother thinks I should call my daughter Mary. That was her mother's name. There has always been a Mary in the family until my gran died. She will be upset if we choose something else for her first granddaughter.'

'I am going to call my daughter Kylie. I want her to be beautiful and successful, just like Kylie Minogue.'

In that conversation you can find the expectations being given to each child along with their name. Just like the fairies at Sleeping Beauty's christening, these fond parents are handing on their blessings and the occasional curse.

You might like to reflect on the inheritance which comes with your name. Here are some possible aspects for consideration:

- Were you named after someone? If so, were there expectations attached, such as that you would replace someone who had died, or that you would be as beautiful as your namesake?
- Which member of the family made the choice? What does that tell you about power and family relationships?
- Is there a family 'pool' of names, from which everyone is expected to choose? If so, is there anything distinctive about them? For example, are they used for either gender (Lesley/Leslie, Hillary) or are they unusual and quirky (Fifi, Trixiebelle)?

- Recall what you have been told about how and why your name/s came to be chosen and reflect on what this tells you about the role you are expected to fulfil in your family.
- Are there any changes in your role (or your name) that you would like to make? Perhaps you want to let go of a diminutive, or a nickname which is disparaging, or has become too young for you, or use a version of your name which is more fun. Perhaps you no longer wish to be seen in the same way as all the other 'Marys' in the family, or as 'shortly-to-be-famous' Kylie.
- Think of a first step to making any changes you would like to make.

Only You

Every time I see a newborn baby for the first time I am, of course, looking at a 'one-off'. We all know that each human being is unique. That is one of the central factors which makes the work of a counsellor so fascinating and so difficult. The historical, social and family factors we have touched on are transmitted to us through particular events and relationships, but babies do not begin life as empty vessels, waiting to be filled with experience. Each baby has a unique genetic inheritance; each has an individual personality structure. Anyone who has had long-term contact with more than one child, knows that each needs a particular mode of care, suited to their particular needs, if they are to be secure and to thrive. My 'nurture' meets with my 'nature', and the extraordinary and unique set of encounters and memories which I know as my life unfolds.

If you wish to test this out, talk to a relative or a friend about an event from the past (the further back the better) in which you were both participants. You will find that your individual perception and memory have combined to produce a unique reading of the meaning of the event, which is tailor-made for you, and may be different in many respects to your companion's reading; sometimes the differences are so startling that it is difficult to believe that you were both at the same event.

Take some time now to look at some aspects of your 'nature'.

Only Connect

Tiny babies experience emotion through their bodies. Fear, for example, is felt as a set of powerful physical sensations – sweating, shaking, heart pounding, stomach churning – before we have words with which to name it. In our adult lives, many of us become 'disembodied' for long stretches of the day. Those of us who live in cities 'switch off' our awareness, to protect ourselves from the close proximity of so many strangers. For much of the time we live in our intellects. This state damps down our receptiveness to feelings in ourselves and others. As a counsellor, my body is an invaluable channel through which I can 'tune in' to undercurrents of feeling, which may not be accessible to observation. I need to find ways to re-form the channels between my mind and my body, which make this possible. It is important to receive these messages from below the surface of consciousness. Through them I can discover channels of repressed feelings which may be greatly influencing my client's life, even though, without these physical signals, they and I may be completely unaware of them.

Take some time now to pay attention to what is happening beneath the surface of your own body.

- Lie down and close your eyes.
- Focus awareness on the steady rhythms of your body: your heartbeat and your breathing.
- Help yourself to relax by imagining that the air which you take in is filling your body with strength and peace, and that the air you breathe out carries away with it tension, and agitation.
- Starting with your toes, pay attention to each part of your body in turn. Notice the sensations in each spot. Pay special attention to areas which are painful, or tense, or where there is very little sensation. My body is sending me messages about my state of being all the time. To ignore them is to tune out the richness of my emotions. When I pay attention I may discover that my body has been telling me to slow down and take care of myself, or to speed up and get on with things.
- Take time to listen to these messages now. What does your aching stomach mean? Why are your shoulders permanently stiff? How did your voice become so quiet? Some sayings to be found in common usage reveal the psychosomatic origin of most of these sensations. How would you describe what is happening in the places in your body which catch your attention? Here are some examples:

  - a stabbing pain (who or what might be attacking you?)
  - there's something that I can't stomach
  - he/she/it takes my breath away
  - *** puts a light in my eyes and a spring in my step
  - my face fell
  - I was gripped with emotion

- Decide how you might take more notice of the messages from your body.
- Go back to focusing on breathing, perhaps; at the same time, picturing a place that is tranquil and beautiful, and give yourself some time to relax.

If you are to be a counsellor, it is important to find ways to stay in touch with the continuing signals sent to your mind by your body. Once you are in touch with your own sensations you are ready for the interesting task of registering the effects of the messages which go between the bodies of you and your clients.

Here is the story of one such encounter. There once was a woman whose avowed aim in life was to spread the warmth of human kindness everywhere she went. She was always smiling and helpful. Imagine the mystification of her counsellor when she became conscious that, whenever she saw this client, she developed a stiff neck. She could see how there were some people of her aquaintance she might describe as a 'pain in the neck', but it was not obvious how the description could fit this paragon of concern and forbearance. One day this person smiled at her counsellor, as she often did, and the counsellor had a powerful impression of a tiger baring its fangs and snarling. This gave her the clue which helped her to get in touch with what her body had sensed: behind this person's smiling exterior lay a good deal of anger and aggression. Somehow she managed to steer events so that it seemed as if she was the victim of aggression, not the perpetrator, but gradually her counsellor realized how carefully this client took control of situations, and cornered her hapless victims until they retaliated, when she was all injured innocence, bemused by their anger. The counsellor's stiff neck came from defending herself against an attack which her body had sensed before she was consciously aware of it.

Personality

One of the things which marks out differences between approaches to counselling is the theory of the personality upon which they are based. Each school of counselling espouses a particular picture of personality structure and development. You can find out about them in the next chapter, on approaches to counselling. For the moment we might briefly consider one aspect of our personality: personal style.

Once, at a conference of psychotherapists, some of us amused ourselves in the bar one evening by guessing the school of therapy to which conference delegates belonged, by the way they presented themselves 'at play'. It was a bit like going to a ecumenical convention of clergy and trying to work out their denomination. The 'game' worked well enough for me to conclude that different styles of counselling and psychotherapy may suit people with particular styles of personality, and that this is one factor to take into account when choosing which training to take.

To illustrate this, imagine four friends who are playing tennis. They are all roughly the same, as far as skill is concerned. If we observe their reaction to making a bad shot we can observe some aspects of their personal style. One may apologize and be worried and embarrassed. Another may blame something or someone; the wind, for blowing the ball off course, perhaps, or their partner, for blocking their view. A third may analyse the error and talk about the 'shot that got away'; in other words, the ideal shot which they might have played. The fourth player may quickly erase the shot from their memory and focus forward to the next shot. All four are playing the same game, but the experience will be different, perhaps radically different for each of them.

Just to start you thinking about your own style try this little exercise:

- Write a 'personal column' advert about yourself, but instead of the usual glossy picture (fun-loving, petite, g.s.o.h., etc.) make yours as honest as you can. Focus on describing your personality, and the way you do things. Here are some questions to set you thinking. All of them are 'value free'; that means that there is no right and wrong answer:

  - If something goes wrong, how do you deal with it?
  - Are you happiest spending most of your time in the company of others, or do you prefer to be often alone?
  - Are you excitable or even-tempered?
  - Do you like to explore every avenue before you make a decision or do you 'act on a hunch' about the right steps to take?
  - Do you make friends quickly, or do you like to take time to get to know someone?
  - When you cook, do you follow a recipe and use scales to measure everything, or do you estimate amounts and adapt recipes?
  - Have you a preference for musicals, dramas or experimental theatre?
  - At school did you prefer arts or sciences?

K Do you enjoy using words articulately or are you more comfortable with images?

- When you have completed your advertisement try to prevail on someone who knows you well to write their version of an advert for you, without looking at yours.
- Compare the two. Where do they agree and disagree?
- If they disagree, what do you think was happening? Do your nearest and dearest see things about you that you do not see yourself? Do you present one face to the world and wear another inside?

Keep your personal style in mind as you read this book. Use it to reflect on how working as a counsellor might fit you, or raise difficulties for you, and which kinds of counselling might suit your personality best.

Learning from experience

So far in this chapter I have focused on the resources – cultural, social and personal – which we carry with us as we move through the experience of living. Now it will be useful to look at some of the ways we learn from experience. From the time of our birth (some would say from the moment of conception), we begin to acquire our own unique perception of who we are and of the nature of existence. Each experience teaches us something about life. Put together, our experiences colour our expectations. Somone who suffers an early, devastating bereavement may be anxious about committing themselves fully to love and depend on one person again, or anxious about ever being alone. Someone who has been at the mercy of unpredictable events – for example, having a childhood disrupted by war – is likely to be concerned with how much control they have over the circumstances of their life. Often counselling cannot change the circumstances of someone's life but it can give them an opportunity to develop a more creative outlook.

Human beings are designed to learn through relationships. If I stand in a flat, featureless landscape, it is difficult for me to have any idea what size I am. I learn about who I am by seeing myself reflected in the eyes of others. Those unfortunate babies who are born into a situation where they are physically cared for, but no one pays much attention to them, grow with their ability to make meaning of life severely inhibited. Without being consciously aware of it, I watch and listen as the people around me react to me and to events, and I use what I learn to form a picture of the meaning of what is happening. So I develop an outlook on the world and a set of 'rules for living'.

Outlook on Life

Our outlook has a great bearing on how we live. A woman once went to a counsellor because she felt that life was not worth living. She was in her twenties. She told the counsellor about her childhood which had been devastated by a series of terrible events. Both her parents had died. She had been passed around the family, but never really felt that she had a home. She managed to get to university, but just as she graduated she became seriously ill and spent a year battling with a life-threatening disease.

'There,' she said to the counsellor. 'Is it any wonder that I cannot find a good reason to live?' The counsellor said, 'Supposing I was to tell you about a young woman I know, who has survived dreadful hurt, repeated upheaval, a threat to her existence, and yet has studied for a degree and sought out a way to make sense of what has happened to her. How would you regard her life – as a success story, or as a failure?' The young woman thought and then she said, 'I would say that she must have guts and ability to have got through all of that, and she must really want to live.' This moment marked, of course, the beginning of her therapeutic journey, not the end, but the change in her outlook made all the difference. She carried it like a talisman through the times when everything looked hopeless and it helped her to keep a little spark of hope alive.

Take time to explore some aspects of your outlook on life:

- Focus on your state of being. Tune in to your stream of consciousness. What is occupying your attention?
- What are the feelings which accompany your thoughts? Can you identify an habitual attitude with which you face life?
  - Are you optimistic or pessimistic?
  - Do you feel you can influence the shape of your life, or does it feel as if things 'just happen' to you?
  - Can you allow the people around you to see you as you are, or do you feel that if they really knew you they would reject you?
  - Do you feel that you have 'missed the boat' or are you still waiting for your 'ship to come in'?
  - Do you have confidence in your own judgement, or do you need others to affirm and support your ideas?

The great founder of the 'gestalt' school of therapy, Fritz Perls, drew our attention to the poverty of our everyday awareness. He challenged us to be more present in each moment of our lives. When you 'tuned in' to your train of thought, I wonder how much of it was focused on the present moment, and how much was preoccupied with unfinished business from the past, or with trying to see into the future. My perception of the world is coloured by these habitual attitudes, in ways of which I am usually unconscious.

A woman, let us call her Charlotte, went to a counsellor to look at her relationship with her mother. She described her father as a 'wonderful man', hard-working and interesting. When she was a teenager he would buy her beautiful evening gowns and take her as his partner to golf club dinners and masonic ladies' nights, introducing her as 'my lovely and talented daughter'. For several weeks in counselling Charlotte hardly mentioned her mother; then she spoke with anger and loathing about her as a hopeless alcoholic, who made her father's life a misery and embarrassed her by getting drunk when her friends were around.

Months later she mentioned that one day, when she was 18, her mother had decided that she was never going to drink again. She cleared all the empty bottles from the house and joined Alcoholics Anonymous. From that day on she had not touched alcohol. This transformation had not led to a reconciliation between mother and daughter. 'Too little too late' was the daughter's comment. She continued to be her father's social partner. After all, as Daddy said, 'Who knows how long your mother will be able to stay sober?'

Charlotte had been in counselling for a year before she plucked up courage to talk about the time she lost the 'love of her life'. He was handsome and well-off and successful. She was the envy of her student friends when he picked her up in his big car to take her out. They talked about marriage. Then, one day, they bumped into an old friend of his who asked after his children. Reluctantly he revealed that he had a wife and three small children. 'But she's not like you,' he said. 'She has no sense of style. All she wants is her home and children.'

Panic-stricken, Charlotte ran to Daddy, who could refuse her nothing. He patted her on the hand, sighed and said, 'Men are like that. You'll get over him.' Then he gave her a large cheque and said that he was sure that she would sort it out. He changed the subject after that and told her about his latest business coup and took her out to an expensive restaurant for dinner. In desperation she confided in her mother, for the first time for many years. They spent hours talking. She decided to end the relationship and through every step of the way her mother was with her. Was Charlotte grateful? Did she see her mother in a new light? Not at first. 'You see, Daddy is so important and busy,' she said. 'That is why he had no time to help. Mother had nothing better to do.'

One day Charlotte was talking about the courage it had taken to make the decision to break with the rich boyfriend. 'Where did you learn about courage?' asked her counsellor. 'Who are the most courageous people you know?' These questions opened the door to a change in Charlotte's perception of events and, eventually, to changes in her outlook. With many tears she acknowledged that her father opted out of close personal contact and difficult situations, by hiding behind dazzling displays of his wealth and importance in the big wide world. It was her mother who faced things and won through. It was with her help that she had found the courage to end the dazzling but destructive relationship with the rich boyfriend.

She was still dazzled by displays of wealth and power; still dreamed of having the smart house, big car and a wardrobe full of beautiful clothes, but she gradually saw that this dream had blinded her to reality. Then she stopped chasing the pot of gold at the end of the rainbow, and listened more carefully to what was really on offer.

If I am to help someone to see themselves more clearly, I must first remove some of the coloured filters from my own perception.

Keep It in the Family

To do justice to the complexity of family influence would take a book in itself. All there is room for here is a small 'hors d'oeuvre'. All families pass on to their children an 'instruction manual' on how life 'should' be lived. Much of it is never articulated. The 'rules' in it are communicated in many subtle ways; by a disapproving glance perhaps, or a special smile. These 'rules for living' which shape life in our original family can feel to us to be 'the way things must and should be done'.

Someone described how, when she cooked a joint of meat, she always cut it in two and cooked it in two separate roasting tins. One day her husband asked her why she did it this way. She realized that it was because that was the way she had always seen her mother do it. So she asked her mother why she divided the roast. Her mother said that she had copied *her* mother's cooking methods. When they asked the old woman why she cut her meat in two she said, 'When we were first married, someone gave us two small oven dishes, and they were the only ones we had. Neither dish was big enough to take a whole joint so I had to cut them in two. I've done it ever since. Force of habit, I suppose.'

In this way we hand on the 'family instruction book'. Sometimes the rules in it still work very well. Sometimes they are outdated and not appropriate for our present lives. Many a long-term relationship has foundered because one partner does not behave in ways which the other considers 'correct'. I once asked someone who led marriage preparation sessions for engaged couples, how she encouraged them to look at these issues. She said, 'It's quite simple; I ask them how they will spend their first Christmas. Almost all of them have assumed that they will spend it in the way which is traditional in their family.' The major celebrations in every culture are times when family tradition is at its strongest.

Take some time here to look at some of the rules your family have passed on to you. Any of the following areas often repay investigation, but you may have a particular reason to focus on an aspect of your life which is not included in this list.

- Choose an area to explore. Here are some suggestions:

    - how a woman/a man should behave
    - dealing with money
    - how to bring up children properly
    - sexuality and how to express it

- Allow some memories to surface of times with your original family, when this topic was at the heart of events.
- Replay the scene in your mind and notice the implicit rules and the ways in which they are communicated. Do the adults agree? Do their opinions differ? Is one person determined that their view should prevail? Do the other members of the family go along with this? What is your role? Is there an expectation that you should take sides? What feelings does this scene evoke in you?
- Focus on the present. How do these 'rules' affect your life now?
- Is there anything you want to change? If there is, give some thought to how you might take the first step in that change.

The role we are expected to perform in our family can set like concrete. We may assume the same role in other groups and be completely unaware that we do so. Of course, unless we know what is going on we will take up these roles in response to our clients. Here are some examples. Take note of the ones which 'ring bells' with you.

- The 'lightning conductor' absorbs all the powerful emotions and lets them safely dissipate. If a family crisis is brewing, no one need worry about things getting out of hand, because the LC can be relied on to get ill, or play the fool, or create an even bigger storm on safe ground – anything to shift the focus from the main danger zone. The 'lightning conductor' counsellor will make clients feel safe, but will not let them 'try their wings' and discover that they can weather the storm in their own way.
- The 'parental child' takes responsibility for the care of the weaker members of the family. They sacrifice a carefree childhood in order

to prevent the family breakdown which threatens. You can recognize them by their seriousness and their willingness to take on any burden. The parental counsellor never quite allows clients to grow up. Sometimes subtly, sometimes directly, they make sure that their clients' attempts to be independent fail. Then they pick them up, dust them down and bask in their gratitude at being 'rescued'.

- The 'ray of sunshine' cheers everyone up and tells them that things are not so bad as they thought. Usually everyone loves them but the brighter the light they cast, the darker the shadow that surrounds it. The sunny counsellor constantly reassures their clients, but does not allow them to voice their despair, their hopelessness, indeed any 'bad' feelings. Ultimately they face the darkness alone, but how can they be angry with their sunny counsellor?

I could continue . . . Here are some more roles. Work out for yourself how a counsellor might behave if they are stuck in one of them.

- The suffering martyr
- The strong silent type
- The solver of puzzles
- The entertainer
- The protester
- The saviour

Motivation

If you decide to embark on counsellor training it must be because you hope that it will meet some of your needs and aspirations. It is worth spending time looking at what they might be. This time I invite you to do your exploration before I write about motivation. It feels important for me not to colour your thoughts by starting with my own. You may want to write down and date your answers. It is interesting to look back at what motivated us at various times, and see whether and how things have changed.

- Why do you want to train in counselling? Write down all the reasons that come into your mind. Do not worry at this point whether they are sensible or far-fetched.
- Now add to the list any reasons you thought of, which you might not want anyone else to know about at this moment. (No one but you will see this list unless you choose to show it to someone.)
- Look at your list of answers. How many are concerned with something you want to give and how many with something you want to receive?

- Now look again. First think again about the answers which are concerned with giving. Is there a link with something you hope to receive? For example, if one of your motivations is to want to help people, do you hope that if you help someone they will be grateful, or admire you, or will say that you have made them happier? Have the courage to be honest with yourself.
- Look at the answers concerned with receiving. Is there a link with something you want to give? For example, you might want to be paid, so that you can help your child through university, or receive knowledge so that you can give of your best and work in depth.

At the start of training, students are often asked the question I first asked you: Why do you want to train in counselling? Here are some answers which regularly appear:

- I want to help people.
- I am a good listener. People come and tell me their troubles. I want to be able to help them.
- When I had a bad time counselling helped me. Now I would like to help others as I was helped.
- My present career does not satisfy me as it did once. I would like to have a career which is worthwhile.
- I have always been interested in psychology. I want to learn more about it.

I would suggest that motivation always has two faces; giving and receiving are always interlinked. If I want to give something, I also want to receive something. It is the motivations which feel pure, or of which we are unaware, which can catch us out. We probably all discovered as children that when someone said, 'I am only doing this for your own good', it was as well to be suspicious, because what followed seldom felt beneficial and often met the needs of the giver, not us. I seem to remember that none of the adults who used this line ever asked me what I needed. They all assumed that they knew best.

The sin of pride, as seekers after spiritual enlightenment have long known, is seductive and insidious. In counselling it leads to a division which is deeply comforting if I can manoeuvre myself to the right side of it. It goes something like this: '"They" (those poor souls who are on the wrong side of the line) are crazy, ignorant, failing, not in control, not one of the chosen ones, helpless; whilst "we" (who are of course on the right side of the line, and have a diploma and five years of therapy to confirm it) are' – well, you can probably finish this sentence yourself –

'sane, intelligent, successful, in control, one of Freud, Jung, or Rogers', or any number of other gurus' chosen ones, with an answer to all life's problems and a pure wish to spread the good news to those poor souls who are on the other side of the line.' That finds a place for the counsellors and the clients, but there are other people in the world, so this line of thinking goes, who do not even know that the dividing line exists. They live in outer darkness, getting on with their lives, woefully ignorant of their neuroses, not even conscious that they too could be on the road to enlightenment. The 'chosen few' shake their heads over them and work out ways to bring them into the fold.

I find religious images coming into this because the same 'evangelistic zeal' can be seen in both. Few walks of life are free of it. When I was a teacher we would ruefully confront this tendency in our staffroom conversations. We invented examples of this kind of judgement: 'My child is dyslexic, your child has a reading difficulty, her child is thick as a plank', or 'My child is sensitive, your child is neurotic, her child is maladjusted (a term which has since dropped from use, thank goodness).'

What is the motivation behind this pattern of discrimination and response? I do not pretend to have a definitive answer and if I did I could prevent you from thinking about it yourself. Fear is involved, a wish to be the 'good one' is in there, a sense of security probably plays a part, rejection of those who see things in a different way to us . . . What do you think?

Even my hopes for my client's well-being can backfire. So often they reflect unmet longings of my own. I might have a soft spot for adolescent rebels of any age and encourage them in their fight against the parental authority which oppresses them, because I have not broken free of my parents' authority. I may need my client to become happy, to walk off into the sunset smiling, so that I can feel reassured that I will not be overwhelmed by pain, theirs or my own, but I will probably inhibit the client's expression of their unhappiness. A client will soon sense that I cannot take it, that what I need is for him to say, 'Every day, in every way, I am getting better and better.' Of course we do hope that counselling does our clients some good. The problems start when the counsellor makes himself responsible for deciding what is good for his client and for deciding how it should be achieved. It is a fine line to tread.

I may be curious about the secret lives of others. I may want to understand what is happening to me, but find it easier to say that I want to help others. I may want to have some drama in my life and feel that working as a counsellor will provide it. Whatever drives me, unless I understand my motivations I will visit them on others, and want them to respond in ways that make me feel good. It might make me feel better for a while, but it will not leave my clients free to choose their own path.

The only way to deal with this is to get to know myself, so that I can feel the tug of my need attaching itself to an answering feeling in a client, and know that I must look at what is happening, if I am not to lead us both up the garden path.

The Unconscious

There is no space here to do the unconscious justice. It is as if so far in this chapter we have set out to explore the ocean, and sailed about on its surface, mapping winds and currents, but we have not looked under the surface. Of course the surface is affected by what lies beneath it, but the connections are complex and often mysterious. I am writing this with the aid of a computer. I know how to call up a 'Spellcheck' or a Thesaurus on my machine, but I would have to put in a lot of effort and study to understand how those computer programmes work. Counsellors who work with unconscious patterns of response need to work hard to recognize and understand them. How do I know that the unconscious exists? One indicator is the common experience of behaving in ways which feel inexplicable and out of my control. In the words of St Paul, 'For the good that I would I do not: but the evil which I would not, that I do' (Rom. 7.19 AV).

Whenever I set out to do one thing and find myself doing another, an unconscious impulse has taken over. When I feel a compulsion to respond in a particular way, which feels like the only way, something in the situation I am in, or some particular characteristics of the other people who may be involved, have triggered an unconscious recognition process. It is as if the scene has been set once again for a familiar drama, which has been played out before in my life, and I unconsciously take up the same role in it that I played in the past. My expectation is that the scene will unfold as it has before. If the 'script' or the 'dramatis personae' change, I may find it difficult to see or believe in the change. This time the villain may turn out to be the hero, or the unhappy ending may become a happy ending, but I may go on playing the drama I expect, not the one which is now happening.

As you have worked on the suggestions in this chapter, and explored your own psyche, you have been making connections between conscious and unconscious. If you reach the more advanced levels of counsellor training you will work on dreams, which Freud described as 'the royal road to the unconscious'.[2] In training you will discover the ways in which all of us repeat patterns from the past and transfer into present relationships aspects of past relationships. Most important of all, every counsellor should think seriously about becoming a client themselves, and having their own therapy. It is there that you will have the best chance to explore beneath the surface of your own personality.

Knowing Yourself

Before I leave this chapter I suggest that you reflect on how you have found it to look at yourself. How would it feel, do you suppose, to spend years in training and therapy doing more of this? As you reflect, keep in mind that a new client, embarking on counselling for the first time, will go through similar feelings. As I learn about myself, I become more able to understand others. The two processes go in parallel. At its heart, that is what preparing to be a counsellor is about.

6
Choosing an Approach

Not long ago I visited a centre for healing of worldwide renown. It was set in beautiful woodland. 'Patients' came for a stay of several days, or even weeks. On arrival they had an interview with one of the staff, who prescribed a preparatory programme of exercise, study and relaxation (the centre had its own gymnasium and library). At night, after careful bathing, 'patients' slept in a special ward. Next day they again visited a member of staff, taking any dreams they had the night before to be interpreted. Treatment was based on the dream interpretations. It ranged from herbal drug treatment to surgery, but for most patients the psychological experience of the encounter with the unconscious through dreams was the foundation of healing. It was known as 'meeting with the god'. It was believed that 'patients' had a personal encounter with the god of healing, who showed them the way through their problems. All this treatment was provided on payment of a sliding scale of fees, which depended on the patients' income. An unusual treatment facility was the centre's theatre, where all members of the community could attend dramatic performances, and have the cathartic experience of observing the drama of life performed with tragic or comic intensity.

The healing centre was Epidaurus, the ancient Greek sanctuary dedicated to Asclepios, the god of healing. The sanctuary was built in the sixth century BC, and 200 years later it had become a place of pan-Hellenic pilgrimage. The 'patient' came to the sanctuary seeking healing of their 'whole person', body, mind and spirit. Asclepios was pictured as a serpent, who, because he lived above and within the earth, knew the mysteries of therapeutic herbs and was in touch with the dark and hidden forces of the underworld. These powers could communicate with the human world in mysterious and magical ways, often through dreams. The priests of Asclepios interpreted the god's messages and prescribed treatment. To qualify them for this work they underwent a process of personal and professional initiation. Their symbol was a serpent twined round a rod, the symbol still used by doctors today.

Walking through the olive groves, I mused on whether we have advanced very much in our treatment of many of the ills that assail us. Of course we have a whole armoury of medical advances, but the basic components of treatment were all there 2,600 years ago, and the healers then were quite clear that a healthy mind, a healthy soul and a healthy body were inextricably linked and should be treated as a unity. It is much harder now to find treatment of the whole person. Knowledge of human functioning has become divided into specialized areas. In the nineteenth century, the scientific revolution advanced on a wave of tremendous optimism. By the end of the same century, better methods of treating physical disease had been discovered and tested. Leeches and bloodletting were replaced as treatments of choice by a growing armoury of drugs. Anaesthetics made possible the development of surgery from something akin to butchery to the many-faceted art it is today. The ills of the spirit were of less concern except to those with deep religious faith.

When it came to the ills of the mind, treatment was primitive and brutal up to the early years of the twentieth century. Most of you will know that the famous 'Bedlam' asylum for the insane in London was used as a kind of live horror show by fashionable men and women. Those with lesser ills were usually cared for by their families, who often locked them away, like Mrs Rochester in Charlotte Brontë's *Jane Eyre*. Psychological difficulties and behaviour which offended against strict moral codes were mixed together, with the result that there are still people in their seventies and eighties who were incarcerated in 'mental hospitals' for years because they gave birth to an illegitimate child or were otherwise deemed to be 'moral degenerates'. I remember someone telling me that his parents had both been psychiatric nurses before the war. At that time, one of the main qualifications for the work was physical strength. It was the development of tranquillizing drugs which made possible the reduction of such physical restraints as the straitjacket and padded cell.

So what led to the development of present-day therapeutic approaches?

Five Ways to Explore the Mind

All therapeutic approaches focus on one or more of five possible strands of exploration: relationship, release of feelings, insight, patterns of thought and behaviour, and the social and cultural context within which the individual lives. Each approach varies the importance given to each strand of exploration and the methods used to explore a particular area. One factor to bear in mind, as you decide which approach to counselling you might choose, is how these ways of exploring might fit or not fit your personal style. It is important for counsellors to have a repertoire of skills which enhance their personal qualities, if they are to be genuine and congruent in their approach.

Relationship

When researchers ask clients to say what was the most important factor in their counselling, the great majority say that a good relationship with the counsellor was the foundation for everything else. This is true of all forms of healing. I remember a time when I was in hospital for four weeks. Every day a nurse would make my bed and help me wash. Some did this task in such a way that I felt cared for and respected. Others treated it as a chore, and me as an inconvenience. They would leave me feeling depressed and 'sore'. The relationship between counsellor and client has several therapeutic aspects. The most important are listed below. Most are present in all forms of counselling. Others may be used as specific tools in some approaches.

- Emotional functioning: At the most basic level, client and counsellor must both be able to establish and maintain a relationship within which feelings can be explored. If, as a result of past experiences, or present impairment of emotional functioning, this is not possible, there may not be a good enough basis for counselling.
- Personal qualities: The most important are empathy, genuineness and respect for the autonomy of others. The need for respect implies that the counsellor must be able to relate to a variety of lifestyles, cultures and value systems, even when they may be diametrically opposed to their own. I do not have a right to instruct my clients in how to live their lives. I do have a duty to help them to find creative and fulfilling ways to live. The distinction is not always clear and so needs careful consideration. I will not help them if I try to impose my lifestyle on them. Most clients come for counselling when they are in a vulnerable state. It is important that their counsellor does not exploit this in any way.
- Clear boundaries: You may have seen the debate in the press about 'false memory syndrome'. The newspapers reported concerns that counsellors may have persuaded some of the people who came to them for help that their problems were the consequence of having been sexually abused in childhood. As our memories of childhood are often fragmentary and ambiguous (was Daddy tickling me, or was he touching me sexually?), it is possible to weight the evidence to fit a particular preconceived idea in the counsellor's mind and thus to convince the client that this 'must' be the explanation for their distressing symptoms. False accusations of sexual abuse cause great distress to the families concerned, but so do true accusations which are met with disbelief and indifference. This is a very difficult and delicate area.

  Of course, if a counsellor engages in a sexual relationship with a client they are exploiting the client's vulnerability, and abusing the power of the counselling relationship. We expect counsellors to know how best to help us. If we are feeling lonely and lacking in self-esteem, it may be very flattering to know that the counsellor is attracted to us, but as soon as the boundary is crossed and sexual activity begins, the counsellor is no longer an objective, professional carer. The psychological consequences are similar to the after-effects of incest. Clients who have been exploited in this way often have great difficulty in going on to form close trusting relationships. The BAC *Code of Ethics and Practice for Counsellors* is very clear about the importance of protecting the client from all forms of exploitation. Section 2.2.6 of the *Code* states that 'Counsellors must not exploit their clients financially, sexually, emotionally, or in any other way. Engaging in sexual activity with the client is unethical.'

- Focus: Therapeutic relationships are focused on the needs and concerns of the client. The counsellor has to find other ways to meet their own needs. It is usually not seen as appropriate for the counsellor to reveal personal details about their life to the client. The more the client knows about the counsellor's life the more likely they are to be inhibited by the knowledge. If you know that your counsellor has no children will you feel free to talk about your own children, or will you be anxious that your counsellor may be unable to have children and that what you have to say may upset her deeply?

- Framework: The use of counselling skills may take place within an informal framework, but counselling is seen to need a private setting, which is best kept separate from the client's everyday working and home environment. A contract is agreed between counsellor and client, which sets out regular appointments of fixed duration, often for an agreed payment. Like the pilgrims to ancient Epidaurus, we set time aside from everyday concerns to concentrate on the journey of discovery and healing.

- Transference: There is one less obvious level of relating, which is a vital aspect of some therapeutic approaches. We bring to every relationship patterns of feeling and expectation which spring from our past experience of relationships. These patterns influence the way we perceive and make sense of present relationships. The special conditions of the counselling setting provide us with little information about the counsellor. This intensifies the tendency to view them in the light of past experience. The transference of past to present is, by definition, unconscious. Transference is likely to be used by many counsellors as a source of clues about underlying patterns of thought, feelings and behaviour. In some approaches its manifestations are directly worked with, as they unfold in the relationship between counsellor and client. There is more about this in the notes on the psychodynamic approach.

Catharsis

The ancient Greeks recognized the therapeutic power of discharging powerful feelings. Purgation of emotions was written about by Aristotle in his *Poetics*. He stressed its importance in cleansing the psyche, just as purgative medicines cleanse the body. One way in which the Greeks obtained their catharsis was through watching dramatic performances; hence the presence of the theatre at Epidaurus. The shape of the experience was important. First a comedy was played to increase receptivity and relaxation, then a tragedy to get to the heart of the human experience. At the core of Greek tragedy is the premiss that the tragic hero carries inside him the seeds of his own destruction. The tragedy is inevitable unless he acquires insight into the patterns which shape his inner life.

My dictionary gives three definitions of catharsis. The first is 'purgation'. The second relates to the form of catharsis experienced by the audience at the theatre in Epidaurus and elsewhere: 'Purification of emotions by vicarious experience, especially through the drama.' The third is the form of catharsis which is present in most forms of counselling, and used in specific ways in some approaches: 'Relieving of neurotic state by re-enacting or relating an experience of strong emotional character which has undergone repression.'

All therapy gives a place to the expression of strong and prohibited emotions. If someone has an experience which was traumatic, and which they do not have the emotional resources to manage, a psychological defence called repression often comes into play. The effect of repression is to create amnesia about the trauma in consciousness, and to remove to the unconscious the memory of the traumatic event and the feelings associated with it. This defence protects the psyche from harm, but creates a 'no-go area' around the feelings associated with the traumatic event. Repression protects the psyche from overwhelming trauma, but the repressed material is not available for the rest of the person's life.

To give an example: When a child is five years old her mother commits suicide. The child misses her mother terribly, but her father forbids her to talk about her, saying, 'She was no good, and is best forgotten.' Life goes on; the five-year-old is now a 35-year-old woman. She works in an inner-city community project. She starts to suffer from bouts of depression for no apparent reason. She goes to a counsellor and discovers that her depression coincides with times in her work when she has come across a child who is in acute distress. The counsellor asks her about her own childhood and any times when she remembers feeling distressed. At first she draws a blank. 'I had an ordinary childhood,' she says. 'It was often boring but not especially distressing. My mother committed suicide when I was five, but my father said that she was no good, and that we were better off without her.' 'But what about you?' says the counsellor. 'How did you feel about her?' 'I loved her,' the client says and then she weeps bitterly and revisits the events of that terrible time. As she does so, her memories become clearer, and she is able to recall her mother's appearance, and the games that she played with her. This release of memories and feelings is cathartic. Later the client described it as being like opening a door which had been locked for 30 years and discovering what had been hidden behind it for all that time.

Counsellors using some approaches make cathartic release their central concern. They may help their clients to achieve this in many ways. Some use dramatic re-enactment; counsellors using the gestalt approach may encourage their clients to engage in a dialogue with significant people in their lives (the client gives voice to both sides of the dialogue, sitting in a different place for each); psychosynthesis counsellors create rituals of remembering and letting go, perhaps ending by burning symbolically significant objects on a fire to signify the end of their destructive power and their transformation into living energy. In other approaches, for example behavioural counselling, catharsis is a by-product of the central process of producing changes in behaviour.

Cathartic expression of feelings can release enormous energy. It can also be overwhelming and frightening. If the consequences are to be creative and not destructive these powerful processes need to be handled with great care.

Insight

The initiate at Epidaurus prepared himself to be receptive to a message from the god. This provided him with an explanation of the meaning of his condition. The vehicle of the message was his own unconscious, expressing itself in dreams. Insight begins with a process of uncovering. What is unearthed may be long-forgotten memories, guilty secrets, locked-away feelings. It is important that the feelings are uncovered as well as the facts. This material is used for exploration and reflection. The goal is to gain greater awareness and understanding; a new and fuller interpretation of the meaning of these hidden treasures. The moment of insight brings what the Greeks called *metanoia*. This means a 'turning again'. Fritz Perls,[1] the founder of the gestalt school of therapy, called it the 'aha moment'. At these moments the picture I have of the meaning of my life is changed, sometimes in a small way, sometimes radically. Often I have the experience that the insight has always been there, but I was blind to it until the moment of revelation.

Means of acquiring insight vary considerably across approaches to counselling. In some, especially the psychodynamic and existential models, it is a prime goal: in others it is a by-product of behaviour change.

Changing Patterns of Thought and Behaviour

You were invited to explore some of your characteristic patterns of response in the section on personal exploration. These patterns become habitual. We move into them automatically, just as when we have driven a car for a long time we are no longer aware of the mechanics of driving. 'Why do you do that?' someone will ask and we are likely to reply, 'I just do. I have always done it like that.' Some of these old habits save us a lot of thinking time and energy, but some are no longer useful or appropriate. Like flared trousers and 'hippy beads' they are remnants from the past and we need to ask ourselves if they still fit us well. I can't get into my flares any more, but I still cherish my 'well-meaning *Guardian* readers against the bomb' badge. In the same way, I am glad to continue the tradition of teaching which I inherit from my family, but there are other patterns of thought and behaviour I learned in my family which do not fit me any more, and need to be changed if they are not to cramp my style.

Some clients bring to counselling a specific change they wish to make, in the ways in which they respond to things. 'I wish I didn't worry so much,' one may say, or 'Why do I always start new relationships with enthusiasm, then quickly lose interest?' Some have persistent thoughts which make their life a misery. 'The lift will stick and I will be trapped', 'No one could possibly love me.' Most can benefit from greater integration of the separate strands of their experience. For behavioural and cognitive approaches to counselling, recognizing and, where necessary, changing these patterns is the prime focus. For many other approaches, these behavioural changes are the by-product of catharsis and insight achieved in the context of a therapeutic relationship.

The Social Context

We all live in groups; family groups, working groups, special interest groups, leisure groups. Each provides us with a frame of reference for an aspect of our lives. We also live within a particular social and cultural context, which enhances and limits our opportunities and shapes our expectations of life. In homogeneous, stable communities there is a shared culture, which is known to everyone. In our time of rapid change in a multicultural society, it is important to be aware of the effects of living in a shifting pattern of social influence. These social patterns form the context for all counselling.

Some approaches to counselling, notably systemic work, focus on interaction between individuals, rather than the inner world of one person. Some counsellors use any one of several approaches to work with couples or families. Group counselling draws on the dynamics which develop between any group of people, to form a therapeutic culture, within which the individuals in the group can explore their own feelings and relationships. A group may have a shared problem: eating disorders, or depression, for example. A group may be a general therapy group, where the group conductor collects a group of selected strangers together, to work with each other. Inter-cultural counselling may be done with individuals, or in groups. In this form of counselling special attention is paid to the effects of culture on the lives of individuals. All counsellors need to learn about social factors and to remember that, when they work with an individual, any change in this person will affect the lives of everyone with whom they live and work. Counsellors also need to pay attention to their own social and cultural attitudes, if they are to work in an inclusive and non-oppressive way.

The Development of Modern Approaches to Counselling

The study of psychology grew from two contrasting fields of philosophy: the romantic movement, with its emphasis on the dark and mysterious forces which influence the working of the mind; and logical positivism, which, by stressing the importance of empirical methods, provided the philosophical foundation for scientific modes of exploration. Thus the mind can be seen either as a hidden and mysterious place, only accessible in the hints and glimpses revealed by paying careful attention to each individual's account of their thoughts and feelings; or as a mechanism, which can be understood by observing the functioning of each component part. At the end of the nineteenth century, there was much debate about the relative merits of the two approaches which sprang from this philosophical divergence; the introspective approach and the behavioural approach to the study of psychology. The argument between 'inside-out' and 'outside-in' went like this:

Dr Deep Thought The workings of the mind are internal. The only way to reach them is by asking individuals to describe their experiences and feelings and to use these descriptions to analyse the internal processes which produce them. Human beings have free will, and can reflect on their actions. Behaviour is made meaningful only when we understand the conscious and unconscious processes in the mind of the individual who enacts the behaviour, and the meaning of the behaviour to the person who produced it. It is necessary to start from the inside in order to understand mental life. Objective observation is impossible, since the presence of the observer influences the thoughts and feelings of the person observed.

Professor Observe and Define Wait a minute, you have not yet defined what you mean by mind. Are emotions, intuitions and feelings mechanisms of the mind? It may be more accurate to locate them in the body's hormonal system. In any case, introspection is subjective and unreliable. There is no objective method to verify the observations produced in this way. How can we be sure that we have free will? Our mind is the source of thoughts, perceptions and memories; that much we can say with some conviction. The problem is, there is no way to observe its mechanisms. The only way that we can know what is happening is through observation of patterns of behaviour. We need to look at similarities so that we can demonstrate cause and effect. If animals or human beings are exposed to threat we can measure the effects of this on their behaviour, and describe with some accuracy the threat response. No other form of exploration has scientific validity. It is necessary to start from the outside, with what can be observed, if we are to understand the mechanisms of the mind.

The debate still rages to this day. Both sides have developed new tactics, but the disagreements are fundamentally the same. If you look closely, you can find these fundamental assumptions underpinning the theory and practice of present day approaches to counselling.

The Psychodynamic Approach to Counselling

Psychodynamic counselling[2] sprang from psychoanalytic theory and practice.

Sigmund Freud (1856–1939) was the founder of psychoanalysis.[3] He began his professional career as a neurologist, and he maintained great respect for the rigour of scientific methods. He became interested in the power of hypnotic suggestion to affect physical functioning. Under hypnosis some physical symptoms disappeared. It was clear that they were affected by the mind, but not in ways of which the patient was consciously aware.

Gradually, through working with his patients and analysing himself, Freud developed a theoretical map of the structure of the psyche and the nature of psychical processes (psychodynamics). In so doing, he revolutionized the way we look at the mind. He achieved some notoriety in repressive nineteenth-century Viennese society by declaring that sexuality was the fundamental driving force behind psychological development and functioning. Freud payed close attention to information which came through into consciousness during his patients' reveries on the couch. He used these accounts of his patients' life events, dreams, thoughts and feelings, and slips of the tongue (now widely known as 'Freudian slips'), to form a picture of their unconscious processes. He fed his findings back in the form of interpretations, explaining the psychodynamics revealed by his patients' introspections. Freud wrote detailed accounts of work with some of his patients in his books. Reading some of his case studies is the best way to get the 'flavour' of his approach.[4]

Freud's theories and therapeutic methods were added to and developed by many gifted analysts, who each put their own stamp on the work. Some developed Freud's ideas in ways which became distinct enough for separate schools of analysis and psychotherapy to spring from them.

C. G. Jung (1875–1961)[5] started as a disciple of Freud, but went on to develop a different model of the unconscious, seeing it as not only personal, but also having a shared aspect, which he called the 'collective unconscious'. He also questioned Freud's 'sexual imperative'. He saw the driving motive force in our lives as the move to individuation; a lifelong endeavour to fulfil our full potential.

Melanie Klein (1882–1960)[6] and the object relations school of psychology focused on the first year of life and its crucial effect on how we relate to the inner world of the unconscious and the outer world of relationships with others. She developed methods of working psycho-analytically with children, as well as adults.

Theoretical Basis of Psychodynamic Counselling In their theoretical training, psychodynamic counsellors are likely to study the theories of Freud, Jung and Klein. The basic assumptions behind psychodynamic theories are:

- The psyche has conscious and unconscious aspects.
- The effects of events in our lives depend on the developmental stage at which they occurred and the fantasies which we had about their meaning.
- Memories of traumatic events and the feelings associated with them remain in the unconscious. They influence our conscious life in ways of which we are usually unaware.
- It is only by becoming conscious of these unconscious conflicts, and

gaining insight into their origins, that we can free ourselves from neurotic patterns of thought and behaviour.

- Relationships have many levels; a working alliance is forged between counsellor and client, in which both agree a framework within which to work. It is also inevitable that, at another level of relating, a client will transfer onto the counsellor expectations and feelings which spring from significant relationships in his past, particularly those with his parents.

Psychodynamic Counselling Methods Psychodynamic counsellors use the 'talking cure' developed by Freud, adapting it to the less intensive setting of counselling. Patients in psychoanalysis have, since Freud's day, usually been encouraged to lie on a couch, with the analyst in a chair behind their head. The patient is instructed to say everything that comes into their head. Psychoanalysts see their patients usually three to five times a week, and analytic psychotherapists often see patients more than once a week. In the less intensive counselling framework it is not appropriate to use the couch, because lying on a couch encourages a more dependent state of being. This may help deeper and more primitive feelings to come to light in the frequent and secure setting of psychoanalysis, but is less appropriate if sessions are just once a week.

At first Freud believed that psychological conflicts could be traced back to a single traumatic event in childhood. His early techniques were used to help his patients bring the repressed memory of this event into consciousness and re-experience it in the safety of the therapeutic setting. The release of blocked feelings or abreaction, as it was called, was thought to be cathartic, allowing the release of the patient's life energy (libido) from the anxieties which blocked it. Later Freud refined his methods. He came to emphasize the importance of insight; of understanding the unconscious conflicts and compulsions behind our responses. Psychodynamic counsellors listen and interpret in the same way as psychoanalytic psychotherapists, helping themselves and their clients to understand better the dynamics which underlie the client's responses.

Freud developed explanations for a phenomenon which had long been recognized by priests and others who talk with individuals in private about the most intimate details of their life. In such situations clients are likely to develop strong feelings about their counsellor; sexual feelings, angry feelings, fear, love and so on. Freud understood that the less the patient knows about her psychoanalyst the more likely she is to fill the gaps in her knowledge with imaginings based on expectations aroused by significant relationships in the patient's past. She will then transfer onto the analyst feelings and responses which come from her relationships with significant people in her early life, particularly her parents. She may then respond to her analyst 'as if' he is her parent. Freud named this phenomenon 'the transference'. He began by regarding it as a nuisance, and ended by using it as a powerful therapeutic tool. Psychodynamic counsellors work with the transference too.

A client may, for example, behave as if she expects the counsellor to abandon her when she is most in need of his help. The counsellor is likely to discover that the client has felt abandoned in this way in the past. The counsellor can help the client to recognize that this expectation is being transferred in two ways; first it is important that he does not in fact abandon her and second, he interprets her reaction by linking it to the past. 'You are telling me that you are sure that I will not be here after my summer break. We have talked about how devastated you felt when your father left home without warning. Perhaps you feel that history is bound to repeat itself and it is hard to believe that I will not disappear suddenly too.' By interpreting transference manifestations and not colluding with them, a counsellor can help his clients to understand the unconscious factors which shape their relationships.

Of course, it is not only the client who transfers feeling in this way. The counsellor too brings aspects of their own significant relationships into the consulting room. That is why it is important for psychodynamic counsellors to have psychoanalytic psychotherapy themselves. They need to have as clear a picture as possible of their own transference patterns. When I experience a powerful emotional reaction to a client, I need to be able to discern whether I am reacting as if it is my mother talking to me, or if I am picking up a feeling of which the client may not yet be consciously aware.

Psychodynamic techniques usually take time. Most psychodynamic counselling is long term (anything from six months to several years) and 'open-ended' – that is the number of sessions is not fixed at the start. The counsellor and client decide between them when it is time to end. It is also seen to be important that both counsellor and client make a regular commitment to meet at the same time each week, with not too many spaces for holidays, etc., and any such planned spaces are arranged as far ahead as possible.

The Role of the Counsellor in Psychodynamic Counselling A psychodynamic counsellor is expected to sustain a multi-layered relationship with clients. It is important to form a clear working alliance with regular sessions in a comfortable and neutral setting (neutral in the sense of being free from the counsellor's personal possessions). If the transference relationship is to be allowed to develop, it is important that the client knows as little as possible about the counsellor's life outside the consulting room. Psychodynamic counsellors are caring, but not demonstrative. They do not use touch. Some prospective counsellors are not comfortable with this rather restrained approach. Working with the psychodynamic approach requires an understanding of complex psychoanalytic theory. This is intellectually demanding. Clients may turn to psychodynamic counselling to work out a particular issue, or to gain insight into a deep-seated neurosis. Some use this approach for developmental purposes; to review their core values and way of life. In the hands of a skilled and experienced practitioner this approach can come close to psychoanalytic psychotherapy. Perhaps it best suits counsellors who enjoy working in depth over time, using an approach which is backed by an extensive body of theory, with space for creative individuality in how the theory is applied.

Psychodynamic approaches to time-limited counselling, to marital and family counselling and to group counselling have all been developed.

The Behavioural Approach to Counselling

It was Charles Darwin who first argued that there was continuity between the mental lives of animals and *Homo sapiens*. His ideas opened doors to the study of behaviour. Early theorists in the field examined the link between instincts and learned habits and the effects of the environment on behaviour. These remained the two central concerns of the early behaviourist approaches.[7]

Most people have heard of Ivan Pavlov's (1849–1936)[8] experiments with dogs. He demonstrated that it was possible to change the behaviour of dogs by associating a reflex reaction (salivating at the sight of food), with a new stimulus (a bell was rung before the food appeared). Eventually the dog salivated at the sound of the bell, even when the food was absent. The new response was named a 'conditioned reflex'. Pavlov's experiments are early examples of experiments in the science of behaviour.

John Watson (1878–1958) is often seen as the founder of behaviourism as it is practised today. He observed that all animals, including human beings, develop habits of behaviour. Watson focused on how human beings learn habits of behaviour which we follow automatically.

B. F. Skinner (1904–90),[9] a Harvard professor from 1948 to 1975, examined the effects of the consequences of behaviour. He demonstrated that a particular response is positively reinforced by pleasurable consequences and negatively reinforced by painful and unpleasant outcomes. He developed influential theories on how to effect changes in behaviour by rewarding desired outcomes and by designing environments which reward desired outcomes. When I was a young teacher in the 1960s, the ideas we were given on class management came from Skinner's theories. We were told that if we paid more attention to children who were behaving badly, they would be more likely to repeat the bad behaviour and that it was more productive to pay attention to good behaviour and ignore bad behaviour. I found that this worked up to a point, but, as anyone who has cared for children will tell you, there are some kinds of bad behaviour it is impossible to ignore.

Hans Eysenck (1916–)[10] developed theories to seek to explain the sources, innate and acquired, of neurotic responses. He formed a theory of differing personality types to explain why some people develop neuroses whilst others do not.

Theoretical Basis of Behavioural Counselling The basic assumptions behind behavioural theories are:

- Human beings are complex animals. Results obtained from observations of animals can be extrapolated to explain human behaviour.
- The mind is a 'black box'; we can observe something happening to the person and watch and record their reaction, but it is impossible to know the process between the stimulus and the response, because it is only accessible through introspection, which is scientifically unverifiable.
- Habits of behaviour are learned and repeated until they become automatic.
- Behavioural habits are more likely to be repeated if they have pleasurable consequences.
- Successful behaviour habits are adaptive; that is, they increase the chances of survival of the person who practises them.
- Unsuccessful behaviour patterns are unadaptive.
- High anxiety leads to neurotic and unadaptive behaviour.
- If someone shifts to more adaptive patterns of behaviour, they will feel better about themselves and their life.

Behavioural Counselling Methods Many of the detailed therapeutic methods used in this approach were developed by Joseph Wolpe (1915–).[11] The aim of behavioural counselling is to work with the client to develop useful adaptive responses to compete with and eventually replace neurotic responses. This is achieved through processes of relearning, combined with techniques to reduce anxiety. Here are some of the most used behavioural therapy techniques.

Behavioural assessment is used to form a detailed account of problem areas and develop a guide to counselling methods which are likely to prove effective. This assessment is a detailed, painstaking process of ascertaining the client's patterns of behaviour, which may include accumulating considerable detail about the client's history.

Relaxation techniques are used to promote deep relaxation. This may be a goal in itself, or an adjunct to other treatment methods.

Desensitization is used when a behavioural assessment finds specific areas of phobic anxiety, rather than wide-ranging general anxiety. The client is taught to relax and gradually focus in on increasingly fear-provoking stimuli, until the fear abates. This method has been used to treat fear of flying, claustrophobia and agoraphobia, fear of examinations and other similar localized fears.

Assertiveness training and other forms of rehearsal of useful behaviour are used to develop less inhibited or less aggressive behaviour habits, and generally to improve social skills.

Reinforcement is used by counsellors to influence clients to gradually modify their behaviour. Positive reinforcement is given through praise and attention and, occasionally, especially in institutional settings, material rewards (usually in the form of tokens, which can be exchanged for desirable items).

Aversion and flooding are two rather more invasive techniques based on the client's wish to avoid unpleasant experiences. In aversion therapy, undesirable behaviour is accompanied by an unpleasant stimulus; for example, an electric shock. The aim is to reduce the likelihood of the client repeating the behaviour. When flooding is used, a client is exposed to their most fearful situation and held there by the counsellor until their anxiety diminishes. These methods are now seldom used because they run the risk of increasing rather than diminishing fear.

The Role of the Counsellor in Behavioural Counselling The role of the counsellor in behavioural counselling is to be non-punishing and supportive and so provide a positively reinforcing environment. There is a strong teaching element to the work of helping clients to unlearn unhelpful habits of behaviour and to acquire more useful patterns. The behavioural approach usually calls for a high level of intervention by the counsellor. The interaction between client and therapist is controlled and structured. Plans of action are formed and tasks are often set for the client to work on between sessions. Behavioural counselling is usually short term and focused on particular aspects of the client's life. This approach is likely to suit counsellors who like to work in a structured and focused way, with identifiable goals.

Cognitive Counselling

Behavioural counselling has undergone a revolution since the late 1970s through the introduction of cognitive theory. Since that time, many behavioural counsellors have worked with their clients' cognitions as well as their behaviour patterns. Cognitions are the thoughts and beliefs we have about our lives. They might be described as our 'internal philosophy'. They play a part in shaping the explanations we form for why our lives are as they are. Essential to this 'cognitive shift' is the basic assumption that human beings are not just complicated animals. We have capabilities which are distinctively human. The repertoire of behaviours of which we are biologically capable makes possible many patterns of response to events. How we do respond is formed by what we learn through experience. This learning is made possible by uniquely human cognitive abilities. We have the ability to reflect on what we do, and to observe what other people do, and then to choose to adapt our behaviour, in the light of what we learn from our reflections and observations. Of course, along the way we are likely to pick up some distortions in cognition, which lead to less useful adaptations in our behaviour. Cognitive counselling[12] sets out to reshape cognitions with the counsellor in the role of encouraging retrainer.

As with other approaches, there are several variants of cognitive counselling based on the 'fine tuning' given to the approach by different theorists. Cognitive counselling theory and practice are so closely linked that I have not separated them, as I have in earlier sections. Perhaps different versions of the same approach 'cross-fertilize' over time and this has yet to happen with cognitive counselling.

The Theory and Practice of Cognitive Counselling Albert Bandura (1925–)[13] conducted research into cognition, and its effect on behaviour. He shaped his ideas into a system of social cognitive theory. He challenged Skinner's picture of the environment influencing behaviour. Instead he saw a reciprocal process taking place, where individuals are both changed by and themselves change their environments. There is thus a constant interchange between social and cognitive processes. Personal freedom is based on our ability to use this interaction in a new and individual way. Our ability to learn is enhanced by specifically human capabilities based on the use of symbolization. This makes it possible to learn by anticipating the possible consequences of our actions, or by observing the responses of others. We can then regulate our responses to produce the desired result.

The social cognitive counselling approach developed by Bandura draws on these human capabilities. The counsellor engages in 'participant modelling'. To help a client deal with a feared activity the counsellor does the activity again and again, gradually drawing the client in to act with them. When anxiety levels are high, the activity is approached step by step. Gradually the counsellor withdraws from modelling participation and the client takes over. The process is complete when the client performs the actions with the counsellor in another room. In education and career settings similar guided mastery methods are used to increase a client's belief in their ability to accomplish desired activities.

Albert Ellis (1913–)[14] grew up in New York. He had two younger siblings, an absent father and a mother who was preoccupied with her own concerns. He had long stretches of illness in childhood. Perhaps not surprisingly he became a shy anxious child. It is always interesting to know a little about the formative experiences of psychological theorists. Their approach to therapeutic issues is inevitably influenced by their own experience. It also gives you the opportunity to see whether there might be any similarities with your personality forma-tion and motivation. In Albert Ellis' case, perhaps it is not surprising that his therapeutic methods should emphasize self-reliance and rationality, as tools to build a personal philosophical framework for life, in the face of uncertainty and misunderstanding.

First he trained as a psychoanalyst. His early interest in philosophy led to a fascination with the personal philosophies developed and used by individuals to guide their lives. Eventually he developed his own approach to therapy. The basic premiss of the rational emotive behaviour counselling (REBC)[15] which he developed is that all human beings seek to achieve basic goals of survival, freedom from pain and personal satisfaction – happiness. Attempts to achieve these goals can be guided by personal philosophies which are rational and self-actualizing (an awkward term which means promoting personal development and satisfaction) or irrational and self-defeating. Our personal philosophy is influenced by learning from our social context, from personal experience and from experiencing the consequences of our actions.

REBC counsellors teach their clients to reshape their personal philosophy in ways which lessen rigid and demanding beliefs and actions and increase rational strategies, in pursuit of both short-term and long-term goals. Change is maintained through homework procedures to check progress and correct 'backsliding'. Clients who come with the goal of freedom from a specific troublesome symptom may have 30-minute sessions once a week for around six weeks. Clients who have more severe disturbances, or who wish to pursue what Arthur Ellis describes as the 'elegant' goal of revising their personal philosophy, may continue therapy, individually, with their partner, or in a group, for six months or more.

It is generally accepted that REBC is not appropriate for clients who are seriously disturbed and have a precarious hold on reality. It crucially relies on the ability to use rational thought. REBC counsellors regard it as important to be able to empathize with both the feelings of their clients and with the personal philosophical frameworks they have developed. The methods used to teach clients to reshape their ideas are direct and forceful. REBC counsellors usually have a lot to say. They model a challenging, disputing approach to their client's irrational beliefs and unproductive behaviour, and they teach the client to dispute their own irrational beliefs. They stimulate their clients to use their own coping skills by not encouraging emotional closeness or dependency.

Aaron Beck (1921–)[16] was born to a Russian Jewish immigrant family in the USA. His sister died and he was seriously ill in childhood. His mother, not surprisingly, became anxious and protective of her son. Aaron Beck was an anxious child. He suffered from many phobias. He was a high achiever, graduating in English and political science, as well as qualifying as a medical doctor. He was initially pushed into working in psychiatry by a staff shortage in the hospital where he worked. He then undertook psychoanalytic training. Eventually he rejected psychoanalysis and developed a painstaking method of researching and testing his own theories and his therapeutic methods of treating psychological disturbances. In this way he developed cognitive models of depression, anxiety states, personality disorders and problematic couple relationships, and modes of treatment to deal with them.

Beck's basic premiss is that these disorders are the result of faults in information processing. In order to correct the faults it is necessary to obtain a picture of the client's cognitive processes and set-thought patterns laid down through their experience of life. Beck called these fixed, automatic thought patterns 'schemas'. If someone has developed unproductive schemas, his information processing systems will be distorted in unproductive ways. Behind the schemas are genetically inbuilt patterns and varying levels of cognitive vulnerability, influenced by the level of stress and trauma experienced throughout life. Beck did not regard psychiatrically disturbed behaviour as fundamentally different from 'normal' behaviour. He saw these forms of behaviour as different points on a continuum.

The Role of the Counsellor Working with Cognitive Counselling The process of cognitive counselling begins with assessment of the client's level of functioning and problematic symptoms, using inventories developed and tested by Beck. A full history provides clues to the development of the client's schemas. The alleviation of symptoms is the first goal of treatment, together with techniques to prevent relapse. The client is encouraged to look at the effects of their underlying beliefs on their life and relationships and is often taught improved social skills. Finally the underlying problematic schemas, from which the troublesome symptoms developed, are worked on and modified.

The cognitive counsellor is guide, teacher, encourager and researcher into the underlying thought patterns of clients. Cognitive counselling is usually brief (up to 20 sessions) with later follow-up sessions to check progress and boost relearning. Rational emotive behaviour counselling calls for an assertive active involvement by the counsellor.

Existentialism and the Existential and Humanistic Approaches to Counselling

Until the Second World War, psychoanalytic theory and behavioural theory were the main reference points for therapeutic practice. At this point a new and powerful 'third force' took the stage in the United States. Existential philosophy[17] provided the basic assumptions which underpin the theoretical frameworks for existential and humanistic approaches to counselling. This added a new dimension to the debate about 'inside-out' versus 'outside-in'. Confronted with Dr Deep Thought and Professor Observe and Define, the existential counsellor[18] would be likely to say:

> I recognize the validity of psychodynamic theory, but I want to draw attention to the importance of social and cultural changes between the nineteenth-century world in which Freud developed his theories, and the twentieth-century, post-war world in which we live. We have different conflicts to cope with now. No longer are we likely to be in the grip of sexual repression. Many more of us have the freedom to choose how we live our lives. We are less likely to live by a fixed set of rules, prescribed by our family or culture or a religious institution. With this freedom we have to take responsibility for the choices we make for our own lives, and we must find our own way to cope with the anxieties which inevitably go with human existence, the most fundamental of which are concerned with death, freedom, isolation and meaninglessness. Intensification of these anxieties is the price we pay for freedom. If we were cared for and protected in early childhood these anxieties may not become intense until later. An existential counsellor will work with them in the present, which is where they need to be faced, and only go back to past experience when necessary to elucidate the present.

The humanistic counsellor would be likely to agree with most of the above statement, but would add some of the following:

> It is important to look at the client as a whole: body, feelings, thoughts and spirit. We need to use all the means at our disposal to effect change. Clients need to experience an affirming relationship with their counsellor, and to be taught an approach to difficulties which they can apply themselves. Then they will be able to find solutions to their own problems without having to put themselves under the control of the counsellor. To this end many techniques can be learned to enhance and utilize the client's self awareness. Physical sensation, dramatic reconstruction, healing relationships, meditation and other spiritual exercises; these elements, and many more, may all play a part in enhancing the creative potential of someone's life. Above all, power should remain in the hands of the client.

The Pioneers of Existential Counselling Rollo May (1909–94)[19] spent an unhappy childhood in a large family. His parents did not have a good relationship and one of his sisters suffered psychotic episodes. He studied psychoanalysis and theology, before obtaining a doctorate in clinical psychology. May was interested in the way we experience ourselves in relation to the biological, social and psychological worlds in which we live out our existence; and how we create our own sense of being in the world in the face of the inevitable existential anxieties which go with our vulnerable and self-conscious human existence. These anxieties can be summarized as the threat of non-being. The crucible in which his ideas formed was the two years he spent bedridden with tuberculosis in his young adulthood.

Irving Yalom (1931–)[20] grew up in a poor Russian immigrant family in Washington, DC. He qualified as a psychiatrist and developed Rollo May's ideas, defining ultimate existential concerns and describing the ways we defend against them. You can get a flavour of the existential approach by reading his vivid accounts of work with clients. *Love's Executioner* is a good example.

Viktor Frankl (1905–)[21] was born in Austria, to a Jewish family. Before he was 20 years old, Freud invited him to contribute to the *International Journal of Psycho-Analysis*. He became a neurologist and psychiatrist and chose to remain in Vienna during the Second World War. He was imprisoned in Nazi concentration camps, where almost all his family died. It was this experience which formed the basis for his interpretation of existential ideas, which stresses the uniquely human characteristic of seeking meaning in experience, however transitory and confusing that experience may be.

Theoretical Basis of Existential Counselling

- Existential approaches to counselling[22] start from the fundamental existentialist philosophical premiss that human beings must define the meaning of life in the face of uncertainty and the ephemeral nature of existence.
- Existential approaches use psychodynamic methods, but to different ends; instead of the 'archaeological' goal of psychodynamic counselling, existential counselling helps clients to deal with universal existential concerns.
- Death, freedom, isolation and meaninglessness are seen as the four universal existential concerns.
- Existential counsellors seek to help clients to face these concerns with responsibility and to find the courage to create a meaningful existence in the face of them.
- Anxiety created by existential concerns can lead to the development of defence mechanisms, which must be faced and understood if we are to deal creatively with existence.
- Three modes of being in the world are defined; the 'Umwelt', or natural world, the 'Mitwelt', or world of relationships, and the 'Eigenwelt' or personal world of individual awareness.

Theoretical Basis of Logotherapy The fundamentals of existential theory apply to logotherapy.[23] In addition:

- Viktor Frankl observed that some of his fellow concentration camp prisoners were able to use their experiences to deepen their awareness and to gain in spiritual strength. He believed that human beings are able to develop their 'will to meaning' and that this is the prime motivating factor in their lives. The potential for meaning goes beyond the transitory concerns of existence, to a deeper unconscious spiritual awareness, which transcends our personal concerns. We reach this level through our deepest relationships, through suffering and through our life experiences.
- Where there is lack of meaning in life an 'existential vacuum' develops, from which unproductive responses to existence are more likely to develop.

The goal of logotherapy is to enable clients to reorientate their understanding of the meaning of their existence in terms which transcend their human lives and embrace spiritual awareness. Symptom relief is seen as a by-product of developing the 'will to meaning'. The focus is on the healing properties of the psyche and how to aid their development.

Existential Counselling Methods Existential counselling is based on the development of an appropriate attitude to the client, rather than an armoury of specific techniques. Counselling is focused on present issues and fears, and their relationship to existential concerns. Clients are helped to understand their defensive manoeuvres and encouraged to develop their ability to make meaning out of the events of their lives, so that they can live more authentically. Existential counsellors may use techniques from other approaches if they believe it will further the work.

The Role of the Counsellor in Existential Counselling Both client and counsellor are seen as being engaged in the search to make meaning out of existence. To this end, authenticity and the development of a genuine relationship between client and counsellor are stressed, and a mechanistic application of techniques by the counsellor eschewed. Transference is not addressed, although the counsellor may use countertransference responses as experiences which can be looked at with the client, in order to help them to make sense of their ways of dealing with conflicts. The counsellor models the search for meaning by working with the client to search for deeper understanding. Sometimes the counsellor may take the role of re-educator, for example, in order to help the client to identify and emerge from a defensive response. In the case of logotherapy, the counsellor may also function as a spiritual guide, although Frankl stresses the importance of not prescribing a particular spiritual path.

The Development of Humanistic Approaches to Counselling The most widely used humanistic approaches to counselling developed in the USA, during and after the Second World War. The war heightened awareness of the catastrophic effects of the abuse of power by totalitarian regimes. Revulsion against persecution and dehumanization was a spur to the democratization of political and social institutions, among them psychotherapy and counselling. A plethora of approaches developed, each with its own adherents. All placed strong emphasis on the importance of individuals taking power over their own lives. In this section I will focus on three approaches which have stood the test of time, and continue to be influential: 'person-centred counselling', 'gestalt counselling' and 'transactional analysis'.

The Pioneer of Person-Centred Counselling Carl Rogers (1902–87)[24] grew up in a large, inward-turned, strict Protestant family. The outside world was viewed by them with suspicion and Rogers had a solitary and studious childhood. He switched from training to be a minister of the church to studying psychology. He worked with disturbed children. This work, together with his own relationships with his loving but controlling parents, were formative experiences in the development of the person-centred approach to counselling, with its emphasis on the healing power of non-coercive relationships.

The Theoretical Basis of Person-Centred Counselling

- Individuals are motivated by the drive to develop their potential to live life to the full (self-actualize).
- Our ability to achieve self-actualization[25] is affected crucially by our subjective sense of what manner of person we are (self-concept), how congruent this is with our actual self, and our perception of whether or not we have a valued place in the world.
- Research into the lives of successfully self-actualizing individuals identified six key factors in their concepts of themselves and the world:
    1. spontaneity
    2. involvement in accepting and mutually satisfying relationships
    3. ability to see things in a balanced and rational way
    4. individually distinctive creativity
    5. not relinquishing personal values in order to conform; taking personal responsibility for their actions
    6. ethical living
- In order to self-actualize we need to experience respect from those with whom we have close relationships.
- Incongruity between the way we see ourselves, our actual self and the way we are evaluated by others, leads in the long term to anxiety and distortions of our self-understanding.

Person-Centred Counselling Methods The crucial factor in person-centred counselling is the quality of the relationship between counsellor and client. There are three qualities which are crucial to this relationship: genuineness, empathy and unconditional positive regard. Relationships which have these qualities provide the necessary conditions for clients to explore their self-concept and to develop healthy attitudes to themselves and their lives. These attitudes will enable them to adapt to living creatively in a changing world. Rogers acknowledges that there are unconscious factors at work, but views them as 'tap roots' to the true self, rather than the troublesome source of instinctual energy described by Freud. The goal of counselling is a greater degree of self-actualization.

The Role of the Counsellor in Person-Centred Counselling The role of the counsellor is to provide a relationship which has the necessary qualities for the client to experience healing of the distortions in their self-concept and thus achieve more personal fulfilment. The counsellor must possess and be able to communicate genuineness, empathy and unconditional positive regard. In other words, as a student said, when she did a presentation on person-centred counselling on a course I was teaching, 'What it amounts to is that counsellors must love their clients.' She questioned whether she could cast the net of her love so wide. This seems to me a fundamental issue for all counsellors, but especially for person-centred counsellors. What is clear is the importance this approach gives to the healing power of relationship. In order for this to work the client too must be able to form a sufficiently open and trusting relationship with the counsellor. The goal is for the client to develop the ability to be their own accepting, empathic genuine counsellor. The importance of the relationship in person-centred work requires a counsellor who uses this approach to be willing to engage at a personal and direct level with clients. It is an approach which may best lend itself to helping clients who will benefit from a healing affirming relationship; perhaps those whose confidence in relationships has suffered in the past.

The Pioneer of Gestalt Counselling Frederick (Fritz) Perls (1893–1970)[26] was brought up in Berlin. His family were Jewish. Like so many of the other theorists covered in this chapter, he did not have a happy childhood. Relationships in the family were tense and violent. Perls became a non-conforming, challenging adult, whose impulsive behaviour sometimes got him into trouble, personally and professionally. He qualified as a medical doctor, and trained in psychoanalysis. He became a refugee from Nazi Germany, finally settling in the USA. He drew on such diverse sources as psychoanalysis, eastern religion, dramatherapy and the psychology of perception in his work.

The Theoretical Basis of Gestalt Counselling

- A human being is a unified organism. Gestalt[27] is a holistic approach, emphasizing the interaction between self and environment, mind and body, mature and immature feelings, and other aspects of experience which are sometimes seen as separate and different.
- The human organism is designed to make the most of every experience in order to achieve balance (homeostasis).
- Demands from inner and outer worlds disturb this balance. If more than one demand is present at the same time, they are organized by a

self-actualizing mechanism into a hierarchy, from foreground to background, depending on their importance to the survival of the organism. In order to meet these demands we use resources from ourselves and our environment.

- Once the resources are found to meet the demand successfully, balance is restored.
- The term 'gestalt' comes from the psychological study of perception. Gestalt psychologists believed that items within our perceptual field are not each seen in isolation; rather that we make sense of them by perceiving them in relation to each other and to the context in which they appear, until the experience forms a meaningful pattern – a gestalt. In the process, the most important elements move into the foreground of our perception and the least important merge into the background. Once we make sense of a perception a gestalt is closed and balance is achieved.
- These psychological and perceptual processes take place at the boundary between ourselves and the environment. Gestalt counselling seeks to achieve maximum awareness at this boundary, to ensure that the necessary resources to form the 'gestalt' and restore equilibrium can be found.
- The self is formed of aspects of experience accepted and rejected at the contact boundary. In order to be healthy it is important that we take into our selves aspects of experience which enhance self-actualization, rather than those imposed on us by a picture of how we 'ought' to be.

Gestalt Counselling Methods In gestalt counselling the prime goal is enhancement of self-awareness. As Fritz Perls put it, to 'lose your mind and come to your senses'. This is achieved by developing the ability to take in what is self-actualizing and keep out what is self-inhibiting at the contact boundary. The client's neurotic responses are frustrated. They are encouraged to be aggressive in taking things into their own hands, and forming strong and appropriate gestalts. Fritz Perls and his followers developed many experimental techniques to develop awareness, including the use of fantasy, dramatic enactment of important gestalts and work with dreams. One of the best-known gestalt techniques involves use of the 'empty chair'.[28] Clients place in the chair aspects of themselves of which they seek to become more aware. The counsellor helps them to have a conversation with this aspect of themselves, by identifying with it when they sit in the other chair. By moving backwards and forwards between chairs and identifications the client becomes more aware of the relationship between aspects of their experience.

The Role of the Counsellor in Gestalt Counselling Fritz Perls was a performer.[29] He often worked with individuals in a group. His methods could be idiosyncratic and confrontational. Present-day gestalt counsellors are likely to be more 'bounded', although the goal of enhanced awareness is still paramount in the approach. Other approaches sometimes incorporate gestalt techniques, particularly the 'empty chair'. Gestalt counsellors are now more likely to accept psychoanalytic formulations of the structure of the psyche. This aspect of theory was the one where Perls drew most directly on his psychoanalytic background. Gestalt techniques can be powerfully cathartic. Gestalt counsellors are comfortable with being direct and interventionist. They are ready to experiment. Perhaps, like the Master, many of them have more than a bit of the showman in them.

The Pioneer of Transactional Analysis Eric Berne (born Bernstein, 1910–70)[30] was born in Canada to a Jewish family. His father died while he was still a child, after which his mother maintained the family through her career in journalism. Eric Berne followed in his father's footsteps and became a medical doctor. He moved to the USA and trained in psychiatry and psychoanalysis. The seeds of his development of transactional analysis (TA)[31] were sown during his wartime work as a group therapist. As his ideas developed he taught them in Californian colleges. Eventually he was refused continued membership of the Psychoanalytic Institute. Although his own methods give as much importance to relationships as to the individual, Eric Berne's own closest relationships seem not to have gone smoothly. He was married and divorced three times.

The Theoretical Basis of Transactional Analysis

- Berne's aim in developing TA was to form a system of therapeutic methods which the counsellor could teach to groups of clients, who could then use what they had learned to become their own counsellors.

- In developing his theory of the structure of the psyche, Berne leant heavily on Freud's structural theory, although he emphasized the aspects of the structure which are available to conscious awareness. He called these aspects 'ego states'. Berne identified three ego states: Child, which contains the spontaneous ways of perceiving the world which we carry from our childhood; Parent, which contains the social 'rules for living' inculcated by our parents; and Adult, our rational analysis of reality. The ego states interact and conflict, contaminate and inform each other in ways which can be creative or destructive.

- Berne developed his theories to examine communication in relationships. He did this by breaking down a relationship into units of statement and response, which he called 'transactions'. (This concept has similarities with the 'stimulus/response' unit of observation used by behavioural theorists.) In each transaction the Parent, Child and Adult ego states of each protagonist have their part to play. The result can be a clear communication (a complementary transaction), a conflict or misunderstanding (a crossed transaction), or a hidden or mixed message (an ulterior transaction).
- Berne believed that our lives are shaped by patterns of expectation which developed through childhood experience and have become automatic. He called these patterns 'scripts'.
- If straightforward interaction proves too difficult we may move to interactions which are stereotyped and pre-scripted, and so less liable to spring surprises on us. These interactions give us the opportunity to rehearse our life scripts. Two common forms of this kind of interaction are: rituals, of the 'Hello, how are you?' 'I'm fine, how are you?' variety; and games, rule-bound communications where both parties to the interaction play out a familiar script. Each player in the game gets some kind of satisfaction (a 'pay-off') from playing it.
- Berne's theories of functional and dysfunctional psychological states focused on the interaction between an individual's attitude to themselves, and their attitude to other people. From this he described four possible life positions. They are: 'I'm OK, You're OK' – the happy state of being which springs from self-acceptance and basic trust in others. The second position is 'I'm OK, You're Not OK', which shows a sharp division between the sources of good and bad experience. This is the paranoid position. The third position is 'I'm Not OK, You're OK' – the depressive position, which has its roots in the inevitable childhood experience of being less powerful than adults. The final possible position is 'I'm Not OK, You're Not OK', which is the consequence of experiencing the world as a fundamentally untrustworthy place. This position is the basis for despair.
- Individuals are motivated by the need for stimulation and recognition. We seek to meet these needs in any way we can.

Transactional Analysis Counselling Methods TA counsellors work towards a limited goal of helping the client to be more comfortable with themselves, and a greater goal of helping a client achieve the 'I'm OK, You're OK' position. This is achieved by helping them to identify their scripts, analyse their transactions, identify their pay-offs and increase their ability to achieve autonomy. The measure of increasing autonomy is the individual's ability to abandon pre-set and rule-bound behaviour and become spontaneous, in touch with their feelings and less fearful of close relationships.

The Role of the Counsellor in Transactional Analysis It is seen to be of fundamental importance in TA that the counsellor and client agree a mutual contract for the work that they do together, and that any changes in what either perceive to be the focus and direction of the work should be openly discussed and negotiated. Counsellors may act as re-educative parent models, introducing more positive messages to replace 'not OK' scripts. Much of Berne's early work was done in groups, and the TA approach, with its emphasis on relearning and self-help, lends itself well to a group setting. TA techniques may also be combined with other humanistic approaches, particularly gestalt. TA counsellors must be ready to be educators, helping their clients to learn to use the techniques for themselves.

Choosing the Approach for You

You can find which training agencies teach which approach by consulting the BAC training directory.[32] Many training agencies offer short 'taster' courses. It may be a good idea to enrol for one or more of these courses. You will then be able to try out the approach for yourself, before you invest your time and money in a full training. Some approaches combine well and you can find integrative courses on which you can learn to combine more than one approach. Generally speaking, this is more likely to apply to humanistic approaches, although an increasing number of courses are including psychodynamic elements. Perhaps it is as well to take care that you do not end up collecting too disparate a 'patchwork quilt' of incompatible techniques. When all is said and done, what you acquire from learning any approach is a particular map of that still largely unexplored territory, the human condition, and an 'explorer's kit' to help you to find your way around. As we all know, even the best maps are only useful in the hands of someone who is able to read them, and has a good sense of direction. So find a map which is user-friendly for you, find a good thorough training to teach you how to use it, and then continue to marvel at the fathomless mysteries of the human psyche.

7
Choosing a Training

Why Training Is Important

It may seem self-evident that it is important to train as well as possible for the work you do, but there are some hotly debated issues about the best way to prepare counsellors for their work. You will not find these set out in the training brochures, but they are pertinent to your choice of training. Here is an imaginary conversation between two counsellors; Charity Truelove (CT), a counsellor who has many years of experience, and a brief training, and Sophia Diligent (SD), who has worked as a counsellor for five years, having gained a diploma and an M.Sc. in counselling. Each of them has taken up a position at one extreme of the debate.

SD   I welcome moves to establish counselling as a profession. Training needs to develop to meet the needs of the new professionals if we are to be respected and properly rewarded for our work.

CT   You can't train someone to be a good counsellor. Counselling is about caring for people and treating them with understanding, and these are qualities of personality. You either have them or you don't. I have worked with many counsellors in my time who prepared for their work in the way that is best: by training in the basic skills and then practising their craft with devotion and loving care.

SD   Counselling is complicated. Counsellors do more than listen and care. They need to be able to understand what the client brings and to know how to get behind the present situation of the client to its roots in the past. Anything less might help a client to feel better temporarily, but will not lead to sustainable change. Extensive and thorough training is necessary to assess a trainee's suitability and to give them the necessary theoretical knowledge, technical practice and personal experience of therapeutic exploration to enable them to do such complex work.

These differences are probably unresolvable. They arise from the origins of counselling. Charity Truelove is likely to have worked in her local community, offering care and support. Some, but by no means all of the counsellors and counselling organizations in this sector are anxious about professionalization. They fear that counselling will become a highly intellectualized activity in which personal qualities of warmth and care will not be valued. Sophia Diligent, and others like her, are concerned that their work should be built on firm foundations of theory, and practice. They look to academic and professional bodies to establish a framework for this. You will find, on many questions concerning good training practice, that counsellor training agencies hold differing positions between the two extremes expressed in the dialogue above.

The Purpose of Training

Everyone who seeks counselling has a right to expect that their counsellor will be working from a firm base of:

- personal suitability, maturity and stability
- theoretical knowledge
- skill and supervised practice in work with clients.

These three elements form the necessary components of training in counselling skills and counselling. At its best the training process offers you a spiral path of work in these three areas with gradually developing depth and complexity. It is also important to be able to relate one to the other. Theoretical constructs need to be understood in relation to your own life experience and you should be able to bring to bear both experience and knowledge in understanding the situations which clients bring to you. A client will only have the necessary resources to change if they:

- are provided by the counsellor with a trustworthy and purposeful setting in which to explore thoughts, feelings and relationships
- can use this exploration as the basis for developing understanding, insight and self-acceptance
- experience a wholesome and mature relationship with the counsellor, as free as possible from oppression, manipulation and competitiveness.

Why Qualifications Are Important

Counselling is in the process of becoming an established profession. Until that happens, there are no legal qualification requirements for practitioners working in the field. All the same it is important to train well and practise under supervision for many reasons:

- You will be doing all you can to serve clients with skill and understanding and to work according to a coherent code of ethics and practice.
- It is important to do such responsible work in a professional way.
- You should work within the protection and discipline of a professional body.
- Regulation is on the way and one day there are likely to be statutory requirements for working as a counsellor which are legally enforceable.

I would strongly recommend that you apply for membership of the professional body for counsellors, the British Association for Counselling (BAC).[1] As a member you will receive the Association's journal, *Counselling*, which will keep you up to date with developments in the field, and you will have access to information on training and other issues which affect you.

Registration

Voluntary registration of counsellors is already under way.[2] The date of the public launch of the United Kingdom Register of Counsellors, September 1997, is an important landmark in the development of counselling. The register holds the names of counsellors who practise independently and counsellors who work for a register sponsoring organization. The benchmark for registration as an independent practitioner is BAC counsellor accreditation, or accreditation with COSCA, the Confederation of Scottish Counselling Organizations.[3] There are three routes to acquiring BAC accreditation, each involving completion of differing proportions of training, self-development, casework practice and supervision. The details are to be found in the BAC training directory. Counsellors who work in Scotland can become accredited with either BAC or COSCA. You would be well advised to check accreditation requirements with one of these organizations; otherwise you may find that you have given valuable time and money to training and casework which have not been done under the right conditions to be counted towards accreditation requirements. For example, you may have amassed enough hours of work with clients, but if you did not have the required number of hours of supervision to support this work, your client work could not be counted for accreditation purposes.

   Many voluntary counsellors train with an organization like 'Cruse'[4] or 'Relate'[5] and work productively in a team for a few hours a week, perhaps doing work in another field at the same time. They will be able to become a registered sponsored counsellor.

A Guide to Training

Counsellor training has three principal progenitors: voluntary organizations; universities and colleges; and psychotherapeutic and psychoanalytic training organizations.

Voluntary organizations offer care and support in the community. Some are linked to churches. These organizations share a commitment to making good quality care and high ethical standards of practice available across as wide a section of society as possible. Their services were and are largely staffed by groups of dedicated volunteers. Some have been concerned to ensure that the professionalization of counselling does not sideline the caring volunteer, who from choice or necessity may not wish to embark on years of expensive and time-consuming training. It was from the Association for Pastoral Care and Counselling,[6] an umbrella group for some of the organizations working in this field, that the British Association for Counselling was conceived and established.

Universities and colleges have been the main source of training for psychologists and members of the 'core' professions (medicine, social work, teaching, nursing, etc.). A tradition of intellectual rigour and scientific methodology has informed their training. Since all of these fields of work contain a counselling element, there has been a growing demand from practitioners for training in counselling skills and counselling to be made available to them. The counselling approaches which have perhaps most easily been adopted in the academic sector are those which lend themselves readily to academic research. Behavioural therapy and the newer cognitive approaches, including rational emotive therapy, are well established. More recently psychoanalytic studies have found a place in some university departments.

Psychotherapeutic and psychoanalytic training organizations at one time jealously guarded access to use of their theories and methods, restricting them to psychoanalysts and psychotherapists who were trained by them and accepted as qualified professional members of their institutions. More recently some theorists and trainers in this area have worked to adapt its theory and practice to other therapeutic work, including counselling. The best analogy I can give is that whilst it would be unethical for a brain surgeon to encourage a general medical practitioner to try their hand at brain surgery, it may well be very useful for the brain surgeon to educate the GP about the way the brain functions and how to spot the signs that indicate a malfunction. Armed with this knowledge the GP may well be able to do some useful preventative work, deal with some of the patient's problems themself, and diagnose serious difficulties more quickly, so that patients may be referred on for appropriate treatment by a specialist.

The influence of these traditions can be seen in counsellor training today. There has been much cross-fertilization. Some counsellor trainings focus on one approach. Some follow an integrative route, covering several approaches. It is for you to decide which is most important to you: breadth or depth of knowledge.

The Explosion in Counselling Training

When I trained as a counsellor, in the early seventies, it was not easy to find a course to follow. Relate (then called National Marriage Guidance) trained their own counsellors from around the country in marital counselling, at their college in Rugby. Westminster Pastoral Foundation[7] had recently started to train counsellors in London, and various polytechnics were training counsellors to work in education settings, but there was very little else. There has been an explosion in counsellor training since then, fuelled by the growth of demand for counselling and the wider recognition that anyone working in a field of endeavour that involves good human relations can benefit from a knowledge of counselling skills. If you look through the most recent edition of the *Directory of Training in Counselling and Psychotherapy*, published by the British Association for Counselling, the most comprehensive directory in this field,[8] you will find a bewildering variety of courses, leading to an extraordinary array of certificates and diplomas, many of which were not in existence in the mid-1980s.

In 1985 there were only: 11 courses leading to a certificate (in either counselling skills or counselling); ten masters degree courses in counselling related subjects (e.g. pastoral studies, counselling and guidance) – none of them in only counselling; one Ph.D. course in counselling; and the BAC course recognition scheme was not yet in operation.

You may find it interesting to acquire the newest edition of the *Directory of Training in Counselling and Psychotherapy*, and make a comparison. It all makes the search for training somewhat of an expedition, in territory which is not clearly mapped. I cannot promise to clarify matters completely, but I hope to help you to identify the landmarks more easily. The *BAC training directory* is a useful guidebook to help you in your search.

Three Tracks to Training

There are three main routes to gaining qualifications in counselling:

1. The counsellor training ladder
2. The counselling psychology route
3. The vocational/academic route.

Below I have set out the routes. The notes are as accurate and relevant as I can make them, but there are no nationally recognized qualifications in counselling skills and counselling, which means that, for example, a 'diploma in counselling' can be awarded by many different training agencies, for courses which vary greatly. (For more on this, see the section on qualifications.)

The Counsellor Training Ladder This training route is often offered by organizations which began by providing a counselling service and developed training for their (usually voluntary) staff.

This is one practitioner's view of climbing the training ladder:

I started training from scratch, with no previous relevant academic qualifications. I was not sure what work I wanted to do when I had trained, so I needed time to explore the options open to me. I valued the opportunity to follow the same theoretical and practical approach all through training. This gave me a coherent basis for my work. At the start of my training I was expected to do some work for a voluntary drop-in centre. After the first stage of training I saw clients under supervision in the counselling service run by the organization which provided my training. By the time I completed training I had worked with a variety of clients, some for more than a year. All through my training I was provided with regular supervision, which helped me to feel secure about the quality of my work. I am now qualified for a wide range of counselling work. I have a growing private practice and work for half a day a week in a primary health care team, based in a general medical practice. The training was all part-time, so I was able to do a part-time paid job to help support my family. At times it was very hard work. As well as attending the course, I had to make time for my own therapy and my client work. I got to know my fellow students well over the years of our training. Some of us have formed a peer support group. We meet once a month to discuss our work, share ideas and refer clients to each other, when we are not able to take them on ourselves. I have a supervisor, who I see once a month. (This is a BAC requirement for counsellors in practice.⁹) I also find it invaluable to share with like-minded colleagues the pains and pleasures of my work.

You do not have to join the ladder at the beginning and go all the way through to the end with the same organization. It is often possible, for example, to do counselling skills training with one organization and change to another for counsellor training. You need to take care about moving between training agencies which work from different approaches. This can be confusing, especially when you are a beginner.

Counselling Psychology Training This is a recent development in the psychology profession. As with counselling, there is as yet no statutory bar to anyone calling themselves a psychologist. Concern grew about the dangers to clients who sought skilled and specialized help and were instead treated by someone with a professional sounding title, who may not have had a day's training. In the education, clinical, forensic and occupational fields, psychologists were required to have completed a first degree in psychology which had been assessed and recognized by the British Psychological Society (BPS)[10] and had also to successfully complete a postgraduate diploma in their specialism.

As the number of psychologists working in counselling grew, they formed a 'special group in counselling psychology' within the British Psychological Society. This group worked to form a 'division of counselling psychology' of the BPS, to stand alongside the the other four divisions (clinical, educational, forensic and occupational). The Division of Counselling Psychology held its first AGM on 6 May 1994. I have noted these events in detail because they mark the emergence of counselling as a new field in psychology. The formation of the new division makes possible the accreditation and registration of chartered counselling psychologists for the first time. As general concern about unregulated professions grows, it is likely that professional registration of this kind will become more important across the therapeutic field and may eventually be mandatory.

This is one practitioner's view of training in counselling psychology:

I have always enjoyed really getting my teeth into something. Even as a child I was curious about what makes people tick. I worked as a teacher for several years, specializing in remedial work. Then I discovered that there were ways to study for a psychology degree part-time. It was very hard work but I enjoyed the scientific investigations and was astonished to discover how much it was possible to learn about people by observing them. I graduated seven years ago and continued my work in school for a year, just to have a break and think about the next step. I knew that I had so much more to learn and I wanted to be able to help adults who were not achieving as well as they might. I realized that I had not yet learned any therapeutic techniques and so I enrolled for a postgraduate diploma in counselling psychology. This leads to chartered counselling psychologist status.

Now that I am a chartered counselling psychologist, I have a qualification which is recognized in several areas of work. Staff in many statutory agencies in health, education, and social work are used to working with psychologists. They trust our academic credibility. I am also planning to look for work in an agency which provides outplacement counselling for people who face redundancy. Such organizations often look for psychologists who are familiar with psychological testing as well as a wide range of counselling methods. I feel that my training has given me a wide repertoire of recognized academic and technical skills to draw on when appropriate.

Vocational/Academic Training in Counselling This is where things become really complicated and confusing. In recent years, entry into higher education has become more open. At one time it was necessary to have A level qualifications in order to obtain a place on a degree course and necessary to have a first degree before being accepted into a postgraduate course. There have been two important recent changes in this situation: universities are developing wider entry criteria, and more people are entering university as mature students.

A complicated system of recognition of relevant previous experience and training has been set up by many academic institutions. These processes are known by the acronyms APL (Accreditation of Previous Learning) and APEL (Accreditation of Previous Experience and Learning).

Some universities are also prepared to provide academic validation for courses run in counsellor training agencies. You will find that some of the agencies which offer a ladder of counsellor training have obtained academic validation for their courses from universities. It all means that education has broken out of the nice neat boxes it inhabited and can be found in many hybrid forms. Degree courses take place outside universities, and vocational training may consist of a variety of practical experience backed up by various training courses (similar in some ways to the 'sandwich courses' to be found in some colleges of further and higher education).

This is one practitioner's view of vocational/academic training:

I started counselling in the seventies and picked up training where I could. I have always wanted an academic qualification and the solid grounding in theory which goes with it. My ten years of counselling experience gave me the necessary basis to obtain BAC accreditation as a counsellor. The university accepted me onto a B.Sc. course in counselling on the strength of this. I have friends on the university course who have come from other related professions such as nursing or personnel work. They have used counselling skills in their work and are now looking to change their career.

I like the mix on the course of research and academic work and practical counselling skills. We have placements practising counselling in various agencies and this widens my experience. I have consolidated the knowledge acquired during my years as a counsellor and I feel that I have several options open to me for the future in the academic or the counselling field. I may do a Ph.D. I would like to look into post-trauma counselling and see what kind of help is really needed after a major disaster. I sometimes feel that people get what happens to be available at these times, rather than care tailor-made to their needs There is so much to learn. I am sure that there will always be something I am wanting to investigate.

What Do You Want to Train For?

Knowing what counselling skills you might need is important in choosing training.

Learning/Enhancing Counselling Skills

Counselling skills training is sometimes seen as only for beginners. It is much more accurate to recognize the use of counselling skills as a discipline in its own right. Using counselling skills in a context where you have other roles requires special considerations which need to be looked at in counselling skills training. Some of them are listed below. I have taught counselling skills to a rich mix of trainees who recognize that these skills provide an important resource in their work. The following list is nowhere near exhaustive: helpers in voluntary caring agencies and church pastoral groups, teachers, nurses, doctors, emergency service personnel, bankers, childminders, receptionists, staff in recruitment agencies, social workers, priests in training. Of course, workers in these fields employ varying levels of counselling skills, for different proportions of their time, but there are several factors they have in common:

- It is part of their work to be sensitive to the feelings of a variety of people and to care for their needs.
- They share a requirement to use their skills flexibly to deal with

everything from everyday exchanges to traumatic events, and all with very little warning.

- The settings in which they exercise their skills may be formal and confidential or informal and public, and they must know how to use both appropriately. (I am remembering the doctor's receptionist who had obviously not had this kind of training. She announced to the entire waiting room the confidential purpose of my appointment with the doctor. That was probably 15 years ago, and I can still feel the embarrassment and anger I felt then.)
- Their occupation involves a combination of several different working roles and the necessity to know where they might be in conflict and how they fit together.
- They share the likelihood that they will only meet people once or twice and so have the need to be able to make a rapport and let it go quickly.

A training which is advertised as an 'introduction to counselling' may not be appropriate to equip you for this kind of work. Look for training which addresses the issues above as well as teaching you counselling skills.

Counselling for an Agency

The number of agencies which employ counsellors in a voluntary or paid capacity is growing. Some provide their own training for the work – e.g. Cruse, Relate, Westminster Pastoral Foundation – others recruit counsellors who have trained elsewhere. It is useful to start your professional counselling work within an agency, as you will then develop your work within a supportive framework. To do this kind of work you need to train up to the level required for the agency concerned. Sometimes you can work for the agency as a student counsellor under supervision while you complete your training.

Independent Practice

It is the ambition of many counsellors to set up in private practice. To do this you need to be confident of your professional ability and experience. Remember that the managerial and clinical responsibility for your clients will be yours. You should become a member of a professional body, such as the BAC, and work to their code of ethics and practice.[11] To work in private practice you should have completed counselling skills training, a diploma in counselling and, preferably, an advanced qualification. Look for a BAC-recognized counselling course. This provides the assurance that you will be well prepared for your work. I strongly recommend that you plan to aquire BAC or COSCA individual accreditation before you set up in private practice. As well as being a responsible way to go about things, this is the level of training and experience which is the benchmark for registration as an independent practitioner. If you look at advertisements for counselling posts this accreditation or an equivalent level of training and experience is often required.

Specialized Counselling

You may wish to work in a specialized field of counselling, such as: time-limited counselling, work with drug problems, trauma care, work-related counselling, counselling in primary health care, college counselling, or residential care. (There are many more.) The prerequisites of training and experience for these areas are many and varied. In most of these fields you would be well advised to complete general counsellor training and then specialize. It would be useful to research advertisements for work in your chosen field and find out what is asked of candidates. You will often find that agencies go for people trained in settings which are already familiar. For example, some GPs look for counsellors from a nursing or psychology background, and often colleges look for counsellors who have trained in an academic setting, but these are generalizations and you will find many exceptions.

Marital, Family and Group Counselling

In these fields the theory and practice of counselling are adapted in ways which take account of the way pairs and groups develop and operate. Some training agencies offer training for these fields of work. The British Association for Counselling will help you to locate them.

The Expressive Therapies

Art, drama and music therapists are sometimes employed by special schools, psychiatric hospitals and in other areas where it is important to encourage people to express themselves. Courses in expressive therapies are not common. Consult the BAC training directory.

Counsellor Training and Supervision

Many counsellors enjoy spending part of their working week doing counselling related activities. I find that my training work makes me think about the way I work and maintain a clear picture of the theoretical elements. I also often learn from students who bring specialized knowledge from their work. Supervising other counsellors brings constant reminders that no two of us work alike. Creative reflection on a case with a supervisee is a process of cross-fertilization which enriches both our practices.

Until recently, counselling trainers were not expected to train for their work, but this is changing. Before you teach counselling skills or counselling you should be a qualified and experienced practitioner in the field you are to teach. If you are not already trained in teaching, look out for courses which will teach you how to work experientially with students. There are also National Vocational Qualifications in training offered by the Training and Development Lead Body. The British Asociation for Counselling now accredits trainers in counselling skills and counselling. Look at their requirements. They will give you a picture of what the professional body regards as necessary for the work.

Supervision of counselling and psychotherapy has recently become established as an independent discipline. You should be a qualified and experienced counsellor before you work as a supervisor. Look out for a diploma course in supervision. These usually take two years part-time and should give you a firm foundation for the work. You might be well advised to work towards BAC accreditation in supervision. BAC require supervisors to have supervision for their work.

Other Fields

From time to time I come across counsellors who are working in a field which is new to me. Recently, on a course I met someone who is employed by aid agencies to go out to locations where aid workers are operating, in order to give them counselling help and support. A friend of mine was counsellor for the staff of a hospice. These encounters remind me that counselling is becoming ever more widely used. If you want to keep your options open, do a good general training, up to BAC accreditation standard. You can always 'top it up' with specialized modules.

Choosing a Training

It is useful to begin by looking at the experience you already have, which is relevant to counsellor training. Go through the checklist below, and make notes under the various headings. If you decide to apply for a course, you may well find it useful to have this information gathered together ready for your application. For each section give the nature of the activity, the time spent on it and the dates between which you pursued it, as well as a brief description of what you did, for example:

Training

Dates	Course	Time	Activity
1992	Listening skills	20 hours	Experiential work in listening and responding

1 Training Have you completed training which covered any areas related to counselling? Remember to note the approach followed. For example, if you have studied child development was this based on scientific research, educational theories, psychoanalytic ideas . . . etc.?

2 Experience Have you done work in a paid or voluntary capacity which used similar skills to counselling?

3 Therapy Have you undergone personal therapy? If so, what kind?

You also need to give some thought to your age. I know that this is something about which there is not much you can do, but you will find that some courses have lower and/or upper age limits. Work out how much time and money you have available. You will find it useful to keep a record of all that you do under the same headings as above. There is sure to be a time when you will be asked for this information.

What Are Your Training Goals?
Give some thought now to your goals. To what use do you want to put your training? You might use the last section to help with this.

Sorting Out Good Training from Bad Training
All good training has similar essential elements:

1 *Quality Assurance*
- careful selection of those who have the potential to benefit from the training
- assessment and confirmation of attainment of level of skill and knowledge
- properly validated qualifications
- assurance of adequate resources and high standards
- training staff who are respected and trusted practitioners and trainers
- a training programme with a reputation for producing high quality practitioners

2 *Content*
- the core theoretical model of the course
- practice of appropriate techniques
- knowledge of human development and personality structure
- application of knowledge to relevant situations
- frameworks for ethical and non-oppressive practice
- understanding of the relationship between counsellor and client
- setting learning in a context – the philosophical foundation and social context of the work
- diagnostic skills
- knowing the limits of your expertise and when and how to refer clients to help more appropriate for their needs

3 *Specialized Elements*
Some training has specialized elements (this is not an exhaustive list).

- psychopathology – knowledge of psychological disturbances
- becoming an autonomous practitioner – becoming able to think for yourself, make informed decisions and act on them
- assessment – what kind of help is best suited to the needs of clients
- breaking new ground – research and development

4 *Training Methods*
- look for a good mix of theoretical and experiential methods

5 *Framework*
The framework in which the training happens is also important, particularly:

- class size
- tutorial support
- opportunities to give feedback to trainers and the training agency on your experience of the course
- opportunities to discuss further training and professional development
- a complaints procedure
- a procedure for appeals against assessments with which you are not satisfied
- a trainees' association which will represent your views

There is an extra dimension to counsellor training which is not always found elsewhere in training. Your main resource in the work is your own psyche and so it is important to prepare your psyche for the work, for the same reason that it is important to get your body fit if you want to run a marathon. For this reason all training in counselling skills and counselling should include an element of self-development and/or personal therapy. The rule of thumb is that this element should be in an approach which is compatible with the style of counselling you are learning on the course, and of a level of frequency and intensity which is at least as great, preferably greater than the work you are training to do.

Choosing a Training Agency

If you have been involved in choosing an educational establishment for yourself or a child, you might think about the way you collected the information you needed for your search. Here are some of the factors it is useful to take into account:

- Reputation: If you know counsellors whose work you respect ask them which training agencies they respect. Look to see if courses are recognized and validated by professional and/or academic institutions.
- Information: Is the training information clear and accurate? Watch out for impossible promises and exaggerated or vague claims.
- Equal Opportunities: Is there a clear statement of intent to provide equality of access and opportunity?
- Codes of Ethics: Does the training agency subscribe to a code of ethics and practice? (The most widely used are those devised by the British Association for Counselling.)
- Establishment: How many people work in the agency and how long has it been established? Many training operations begin with one or two people who have abundant energy and enthusiasm and are able pioneers. You may like the idea of being in at the exciting beginning, but take care that you are not investing in a fly-by-night venture.
- Testing the Water: You will invest a good deal in your training, so it is a good idea to 'try before you buy'. Many training agencies run one- or two-day introductory courses or open days. These give you the opportunity to get a feel for the training they offer.

Choosing a Course

It is my experience that many people suffer unnecessary frustration and disappointment because they make unsuitable applications. The old teacher's instruction on exams applies here: 'Read the papers and then read them again.' In some parts of your reading you need to obtain a clear picture of the facts. This is particularly true of the prerequisites you need in order to apply for the course. There is little point in applying without them, if the information states clearly and unambiguously that they are necessary, yet each year many people do just that and receive a disappointing refusal. With other information it can be useful to develop the ability to read between the lines and to look out for what has not been said. There are diplomas offered under the aegis of some very strange validating bodies. Counselling skills training in particular is a large, rapidly expanding and lucrative market. If the bubble bursts you do not want to hold a qualification given by a training body which had a brief and quickly forgotten existence.

Here is a checklist of points to look out for when you are choosing a course. All reputable, well-run training agencies should provide you with information on all these aspects of training.

- Prerequisites: What conditions must you fulfil to be eligible for the course, including any age restrictions?
- Access: Is there a clearly stated equal opportunities policy? Can the course accommodate you if you have a disability?
- Staff/Student Ratio: If a trainer has too many students to cope with, you will get little individual attention. If there are too few students you will not have such a rich experience. You also need to bear in mind the size of group in which you feel able to join in discussions comfortably.
- Content: Compare what is on offer in different organizations. Look out for 'thin' or vague contents or impossible promises. Appropriateness is important too. Ask yourself 'Would I learn what I feel I need to know?'
- Training Methods: As the song says, 'It ain't what you do, it's the way that you do it, that's what gets results.' All training in this area should have a large hands-on (usually known as experiential) element. Correspondence courses are only suitable as general introductions to the area and, even then, face-to-face training is infinitely preferable.
- Personal Growth: All courses should provide a place for this. Usually this takes the form of a 'self-development group' session (or something similar) built into the course. Some courses include what happens in the group in the assessment process; others keep it confidential. It is important to know which. Is the group led by a trained group conductor, or by the same people who teach the seminars? The skills required are not the same, and working with the same person assuming the two different roles is confusing.

On some counselling courses you are required to undertake personal therapy. Where this is required the training organization is also likely to stipulate what kind of therapy you have, and the kind of therapist you should find. You need this information before you embark on your training therapy, in order to save you the upheaval of having to change therapists. Where therapy is not a requirement of the course you may consider undertaking it of your own volition, to meet your personal needs and to give you experience of being a client. The experience of being 'in the other seat' is an invaluable way to give you a deeper insight into the counselling experience.

- Reading, Written Work and Presentations: All courses except the briefest introductions require you to demonstrate that you have learned something by setting assignments for you to complete. If you have not had experience of reading academic books and preparing essays, or you have to contend with a difficulty in this area, like dyslexia, you will have extra reason to find out what is expected of you. You may be able to find short courses or an access course where you can gain practice in these skills.

- Qualifications: What will you get in return for all your efforts? Again, look carefully at which organization validates the qualification.

- Flexibility: There are an increasing number of modular courses available. If you cannot easily predict your future plans you may want to consider the greater flexibility they can provide. It is also useful to check the provision for unforeseen interruptions to your training. Most agencies will want you to repeat all or part of a year you did not complete. Courses change, and many organizations will restrict the length of the time you can take between leaving the course and rejoining it.

- Cost: The course fee should be clear, with no 'hidden extras'. You will also need to take into account the cost of any therapy you are required to undertake and books you may be expected to buy. It is not easy to get financial help for this kind of training, but the training agency should be able to supply you with information about this, if you ask them, and so will the British Association for Counselling.

Course Qualifications

The development of course qualifications is related to the ways in which counsellor training began. There are three kinds of organization which validate courses in counselling skills and counselling. Each has its own priorities and each has a particular sphere of influence.

1 Professional Associations The British Association for Counselling and The British Psychological Society are the main bodies in this field. Both have a system for assessment and recognition of courses in counselling. There is much cross-fertilization betwen these bodies and professional associations for psychotherapy. The main bodies in this field are The United Kingdom Council for Psychotherapy[12] and the British Confederation of Psychotherapists.[13] Professional associations are concerned with high standards of professional practice, and this is their first priority in validating courses.

2 Voluntary Counselling Agencies In the beginning some counselling agencies developed training for their own counselling teams. Relate is one of the best known. Other voluntary agencies, such as Westminster Pastoral Foundation, were founded with the purpose of providing high quality counselling and training. Some agencies, continue to train only their own counsellors; others have opened up their training to people who may never work for them after they qualify. They offer their own qualifications. In these organizations there is close contact and constant feedback between the counselling and training operations. Generally students see clients for the organization and so develop tried and tested modes of practice. The reputation of the training is linked with the reputation of the counselling service.

3 Academic Institutions Vocational training for the 'caring professions' has usually been provided by colleges and universities. As the counselling profession has developed, counsellor training agencies have formed partnerships with academic institutions and sought validation for their qualifications either from the colleges themselves, or from the examining boards which provide national validation of qualifications. Many of these partnerships provide useful cross-fertilization between areas of expertise and give more weight to the qualification given. In some cases, however, the training agency may have acquired academic validation for a course which does not meet the requirements for validation by a professional body. Not all degree courses are recognized by the British Psychological Society. Few degrees or postgraduate diplomas in counselling are recognized by BAC.

When you look for a counselling skills course, check that it has a coherent practical framework, sufficient hours (most counselling courses require that you complete at least 90 hours of skills training) and the opportunity for personal growth. Recognition of skills courses by professional bodies has been slow in developing, because of the difficulties of setting standards across such a wide range of courses. BAC are working on this. Look out for BAC recognition of counselling skills courses.

When you are looking for counsellor training, ideally find a course which will give you a qualification which has academic validation, is recognized by a professional body and provides you with varied, well-supported opportunities of working with clients.

Membership of a Graduate Body

The trainees and graduates of some counsellor training agencies join the professional body related to that agency as trainee and professional members. This professional body represents their professional interests, provides them with opportunities for continued professional development and provides a code of ethics and practice for their work. The professional body may also help put members in touch with work opportunities as well as provide a general supportive network. In a largely freelance profession this peer support can be invaluable.

Testing the Water

You will discover that when you apply for a counselling skills course, one of the prerequisites is likely to be that you have some experience of work which uses counselling skills. Some applicants are frustrated to find this. They feel caught in a 'chicken and egg' situation. 'How can I gain experience if I am not trained? Is it irresponsible to expect me to do this?' The confusion is understandable, but the requirement is important. You and your fellow students will get much more out of the course if you can relate your learning to practical experience. Some people have access to this in the course of their existing paid or voluntary work. If this does not apply to you, an alternative route is to look for a voluntary agency which does this kind of work in the community. Some useful places to find information about these organizations are:

- your local volunteer centre (if there is one)
- the public library
- television programmes which publicize opportunities for volunteering
- Citizens' Advice Bureaux
- newspaper features on volunteering.

You should look for an organization which will prepare and support you well. Here is a checklist of the necessary provision:

- Training: Basic training for the work. (This training will usually be fairly brief.)
- Supervision: There should be regular opportunities to discuss your work with an experienced practitioner. Occasional telephone contact is not adequate.

- Support: Ask who cares for the well-being of the volunteers. The organization must provide insurance, to cover you for professional indemnity and for physical injury.
- Facilities: There should be adequate premises, with safety provision. (This should include the expectation that there will be someone else on the premises while you are working.)
- Guidelines: The organization should provide you with practice guidelines, including a legal and ethical framework and rules of confidentiality.

All this may seem very laborious, but all your practice should take place in a setting which accustoms you to proper working standards and offers you care and support for the responsible and taxing work you do.

Here are some national organizations which use this kind of volunteer help. The address and telephone number of your local branch should be in the telephone directory for your area:

- Mind: Care and support for those with mental illness and their families.
- Victims' Support: Working to help victims of crime.
- Samaritans: For the lonely and suicidal. (NB from the point of view of your future training it is more useful to gain experience in a branch which does work face-to-face with clients, as well as on the telephone.)
- Hospices and some hospitals: use volunteers to give support to patients and their families.
- Support Groups: There are voluntary support groups working in various specific areas, often related to a specific illness or disability. Some require their volunteers to have personal or family experience of the condition, others are happy for help from interested volunteers (e.g. the Terrence Higgins Trust has a 'Buddy' scheme, providing voluntary befrienders for people who are HIV-positive or who have developed AIDS).

In addition there are, of course, many local groups doing this kind of work.

A word of caution: We are often drawn to a particular area of work by our own experience of life. If I have been through a traumatic bereavement, I may be strongly drawn to help others who are in the same boat. If this is true of you, it is important to give some thought to how it might affect you to be faced with constant reminders of your pain. If you are likely to be overwhelmed with pain yourself it will be difficult to pay attention to someone else's needs. Your experience may be so powerful that it is hard for you to imagine that someone else could have a similar experience but need to deal with it in a different way. You may become overwhelmed by the amount of suffering you see and not be able to leave the work behind and relax.

If you have been through a particularly traumatic time which still causes you a good deal of pain, it may be better to give yourself more time to recover before you get involved in counselling work at all, or it may be safer to do general work than focus on a particular area.

Approaches to Counselling

Before you set out to find a training course you will find it useful to read the chapter on approaches to counselling. It is important to choose an approach which suits your personal strengths. This is likely to provide you with the opportunity to use fully your creative potential.

Personal Extras

These are indefinable. Each training agency has its own particular 'flavour'. Some are informal and 'homely', others are large and more structured. Some regard the role of trainers as that of your guide and mentor through a body of knowledge and expertise. Others teach a core body of knowledge and then work out the rest of the programme in a democratic process involving staff and students, each stating what they wish to give and receive. (Such courses are quite rare.) In some, the staff set up the framework of the training programme but there is some discussion about how it is achieved and students contribute knowledge from their own areas of expertise. If you want to try before you buy, enrol for a short course in the agency of your choice and see whether it feels like a good place for you to be.

The Selection Process

Almost all courses require you to attend a selection event of some kind. This will vary in length, stringency and complexity depending on the type of course. In the process of selection you may face one or more individual interviews and/or group sessions. Selectors will be looking at differing combinations of factors. The following notes are intended to help you to prepare yourself for selection procedures, so that you can embark on them better equipped for what can be a stressful process. They are general notes and, of course, I cannot guarantee that if you follow my suggestions you will be successful. Counsellor training is very popular and there is considerable competition for course places.

A Selection Interview
S = selector *C* = candidate

S Thank you for your application. Please tell me why you have decided to apply for this course at this time.

C I have been thinking of doing counsellor training for some time. I am looking at the possibility of changing career and becoming a counsellor, but that is looking ahead at least five years. Meanwhile I use counselling skills in my work, nursing in a hospice, and I sometimes feel that I could serve the patients and their relatives better if I understood more about some of their reactions.

S Can you give me an example?

C Well, I have a patient at the moment who is dying. He is in a very bad way, but he often talks about what he will do when he gets well. His family mostly go along with this but his wife gets very distressed. I feel that she wants to talk about him dying but can't find a way to do so. I would like to be able to help them both, but I don't know how.

At this point the selector is likely to ask a bit more about work, what is most satisfying/least satisfying about it, looking for sensitivity and appropriate concern without over-fussiness. The selector may also ask the candidate what she thinks might be happening in the family she has described, to get a sense of whether she reflects on what she observes.

S Tell me a bit about your life; your family, significant events.

C I was an only child. My parents were in their forties when I arrived. They were both busy professional people. My childhood was uneventful. The days went by in a regular routine. The big moment was when I started school. It would not be an exaggeration to say that it was a traumatic moment. I had had very little to do with other children. I think I took one look at them and withdrew from the sheer overwhelming racket, from being close to so many bodies. I attached myself to the teacher and became her little helper. All through my childhood I found it much easier to be with adults than with other children. It seemed OK until I began my nurse's training. Most of the other students were having a good time. I used to sit in the nurses' home and read and kid myself I didn't mind. Then, much to my surprise, one of the quieter doctors asked me out. I went out with the doctor but I started to have terrible anxieties. They were mostly focused on my body. I was desperate and miserable and so I went to see a counsellor. I went through all this stuff with her, otherwise I don't know what would have become of me. That's how I know that counselling works.

At this point the selector is getting a picture of how well the candidate knows herself and how open she is to recognizing and taking responsibility for her own feelings and relationships. She should have noticed that the gender of the doctor with whom the candidate went out is not specified and should not have fallen into the trap of assuming that she is heterosexual. She has also discovered that the candidate has first-hand experience of the efficacy of counselling.

I have tried in this excerpt to give you a feel of some of the likely areas to be covered and the level at which you might be expected to talk about yourself. I hope that you can see that this is not curiosity, but a line of enquiry relevant to the purpose of the selection process. Of course the selector will also ask practical questions, to discover whether it is practicable for you to do the course. You should also be given information about the training and a chance to ask questions. Selection processes vary, of course, but below are some of the common elements to be found in many of them:

- Motivation: Why do you want to do this training at this time? It would be an unusual selector who did not ask you about this. Saying that you want to help people is a common response, but you should be prepared to expand on it. After all, it could be that this means that you would like to be 'Lady Bountiful', dispensing care to 'those less fortunate' in order to make you feel good. It is important to look at what is in it for you as well as your clients.
- Stability: Have you got the time, energy, and support you will need to be able to cope with the rigours of training? The selectors will want to know if you can 'take the pace' at this point in your life. If you have been through traumatic events, or have had times when you have been seriously depressed, or anxious, or if you have struggled to overcome an addiction, or otherwise been through the psychological mill, this will not necessarily exclude you from training. In fact you may have learned a good deal in the process that helps you to understand the human condition. The selector will want to know how you dealt with these situations, and whether you have been able to use them to achieve a new equilibrium. This is in order to establish whether you have the psychological stability to work with the traumas and pain of others.

All of us need people on whom we can rely to be there for us when we need encouragement and support. A selector is likely to ask about your support system. There will certainly be times during the course when you will need to rely on your very own 'supporters' club'.

Counsellors need to be able to be consistently available for their clients. If you have commitments, e.g. to spend long periods away from home, or a recurring illness which may take you out of circulation at times, or any other factor in your life which would make it difficult for you to make a consistent time commitment, it is important that you give some thought to the necessary limitations this may impose on any counselling work you may undertake. You need to be prepared to show that you are aware of the implications, and have some creative strategies in mind to deal with them.

- Personal Suitability: Of course, a selector will be reflecting on how it might be to be counselled by you. I was once left speechless by a prospective student who spent several minutes carefully assuring me that she was very keen to learn how to help others to talk about their problems, but that when she had a problem she never talked about it to a soul because she didn't need anyone's help. She did not get a place on the course. Perhaps the most important personal qualities to show at selection are genuineness and self-awareness. Any 'phoniness' will trouble a selector. They will wonder what you are hiding. You will not be expected to have everything worked out about yourself or counselling. After all, what would be the point of training if you had?

Group Selection Interviews

Group Interview Some training agencies conduct selection interviews with groups of candidates, rather than individuals. Selectors will probably be looking at motivation, stability and suitability, as in the individual interviews, but they will also be observing how you interact with the rest of the group. They will be interested in whether you can achieve a reasonable balance between contributing and listening to the contributions of others and whether you are able to make a place for yourself without trying to dominate and control the discussion.

Group Case Discussions It is sometimes important for the selectors to know that you can reflect on a counselling situation. You will be given brief information about an invented 'client' and invited to discuss the case with a group of your fellow candidates. You may find it helps if you don't try to find answers in this situation. It can feel as if you are meant to come up with ways to sort out the 'client's' life. It may be more useful to reflect on the important issues raised by the 'client' and the feelings expressed by them, and talk about the questions and reactions evoked in you by this material.

A Final Word on Selection

You will get more marks for honesty than deception, however cleverly done. The selector is not expecting you to be a perfectly adjusted member of the human race but will be interested in how well you know your strengths and weaknesses. Finally it is counter-productive to present yourself as a totally unselfish person, dedicated wholly to the service of others. It will be clear that you are deluding yourself.

Go for It!

All this information may be feeling very daunting. As I write all these checklists I have a picture of the first ever session of the counselling skills course with which I began my training. I was so excited by the doors it began to open for me that it quickly became the high point of my week. I began to see the people around me in a new light. I still find it all fascinating.

If you want to train in counselling skills or counselling then go for it! You may or may not use what you learn to work in 'the therapy business'. What is certain is that you will discover a good deal about what makes people 'tick', where our feelings come from, why we behave in the way we do, how our past experience affects our lives today, how relationships flourish or get into trouble, how we deal with loss and disaster, what makes us psychologically distressed . . . and much more besides. You will meet some very interesting people along the way too, but I would say that, wouldn't I? Training in counselling is training in living and that is never wasted.

8
Practising Counselling

I vividly remember the experience of learning to drive. Like many learners I began with a driving instructor in a dual-control car. I was often glad of his help as I tried the seemingly impossible tasks of changing gear, watching the other traffic and steering round a corner all at the same time. I felt so clumsy and often ended a lesson wondering if I would ever be able to get it all together. I learned the *Highway Code* and passed the test at the second try. Driving on my own seemed an awesome responsibility. Mentally, for a while, I kept the driving instructor beside me. 'Remember,' he said in my mind, 'mirror, signal, manoeuvre.' I got used to driving around the familiar streets of my home town. Then I braved the motorway. There were landmark events: negotiating a multi-storey car park, driving through the narrow lanes of Cornwall, climbing the dizzying hairpins of the Kirkstone Pass, in the Lake District. I really thought I could call myself a driver when I successfully negotiated the fast, crowded circuit of Hyde Park Corner.

The landmarks of acquiring skills in counselling are similar. At each stage it is important to be clear-sighted about the level of your capabilities and not to practise beyond them. That way you can minimize the dangers for yourself and others, and have the satisfaction of working with steadily increasing competence. In this chapter I describe the usual landmarks in practising counselling. At times you may become impatient, and be tempted to skip a step, but the stronger the foundations you build the better you will be equipped to deal with the counselling equivalent of hairpin bends and the more satisfaction you will have in a job well done. The next section takes you through the stages you should follow in developing your ability to practise.

Practising Counselling Skills and Counselling

All counsellors begin by training in counselling skills. This is the equivalent of learning the basic procedures of driving. There are two ways to practise counselling skills; one by doing simulated practice sessions, or parts of sessions, in a course seminar with your fellow students, and two by working in a paid or voluntary setting where practising counselling skills is a necessary part of the work. When you are practising on a course your efforts should be assessed by you, by your fellow students and by the trainer, to ensure that you develop good habits of work. The necessary conditions for practising counselling skills in a work setting are set out in the chapter on choosing a training. It is important that you are supervised and supported in this work.

Here is a would-be counsellor talking about his experience of counselling skills practice:

> I have worked as an accountant for 15 years, so I had always had to try to understand people and deal with them sensitively. Just before I started the counselling skills course I joined my church's 'care team'. We help the vicar with the pastoral work in the parish. I help out twice a week with the lunch club and drop-in centre we run for people who are lonely or housebound. We get young people, some of them disabled; and older people, most of whom live alone. At first I didn't know what to say to the young chap with cerebral palsy who comes, or to the old woman who seems to moan about everything, but I watched the other helpers and took my time and now I find it easier. All the helpers meet once a week to talk about the work and swop ideas. I find that very useful.
>
> On the course we do role-plays. At first we concentrated on one thing, listening or body language; something like that. Now we're at the end of the second term we do longer sessions and try to put everything that we have learned together. Occasionally I lose it and feel very clumsy. Then I talk to the student who was my 'client' in the role-play and they tell me where I went wrong and we work on different ways I could have used my skills. I thought at first that it would be like listening to a friend, but the further I go, the more I find there is to it.

Gaining Counselling Experience as a Trainee Counsellor

Once you have acquired a counselling skills qualification you are ready to find a place on a counsellor training course. On this course you will, of course, need opportunities to build on the basic skills and learn more complicated procedures. It is at this point that you will be introduced to the particular counselling approach(es) taught on the course you have chosen. There will be more role-plays, perhaps with video recordings, so that you can see yourself at work. You will be amazed to discover how many strange mannerisms and quirks you have acquired, without even knowing that you had them. I discovered that I showed impatience by tapping on the wooden arm of my chair with a ring I was wearing. It sounded like a busy woodpecker at work, very embarrassing. That is one bad habit I quickly dropped.

At some point on the course you will work with your first real clients. This is an exciting moment. It is more likely to be a fulfilling experience for you and the client if you are well prepared for it and the client has been selected as suitable to be seen by a counsellor with your level of skill and experience. The agency which supplies you with clients needs to give careful thought to providing you with a safe and supportive framework for your work. In this section I help you to be aware of some of the ways that this should be done.

Before you start client work, the training agency should have carefully assessed each student individually to check that you are ready for this work. The source of clients depends on whether the training agency also runs a counselling service. If it does, you are likely to be provided with some or all of your clients from this service. (Cruse, Relate and Westminster Pastoral Foundation are three of the best-known national agencies which work in this way.) If you do your course in an organization which is purely concerned with training, you will gain your client experience through counselling placements. It is more common for counsellor training to take place in agencies which only offer training. We need to look at what each type of counselling practice provision entails.

Working as a Student with an 'In-House' Counselling Service The training and counselling departments of the organization will liaise to ensure that students are supplied with clients who are suitable for them to work with, at the level of skill and experience they have reached. They will have mutually agreed guidelines for how students are to do the work and how to deal with such practical details as keeping notes, and on ethical concerns such as confidentiality. The clients are likely to have been assessed by the organization's specially trained intake counsellors to ensure that they will be able to benefit from counselling and to ascertain whether they need general or highly specialized care, and whether they are suitable for students to work with under supervision. If you are expected to do this intake assessment yourself you should be trained in this specialized skill. At its best, gaining your experience in-house can provide a rich and coherent progression of experience. At its worst you can wind up competing with your fellow students for a scarce supply of suitable clients.

Working as a Student on a Training Placement On some courses students are supplied with suitable training placements; on other courses you will be expected to find them for yourself. In both cases the training agency should give you and the placement counselling agency clear rules about how the work is to be done. Of course the placement agency will have its own rules for its counselling service and there may be conflicts to be sorted out. For example, on some training courses you may be expected to audio-tape your sessions with clients, but the counselling service where you have your placement may not be happy about the possible effects on confidentiality of taping. If you and your clients are to be appropriately cared for, and protected from harm, it is important that there is a written agreement between you, the counselling agency and the training agency about how the client work is to be managed, and where responsibility lies. At its best, working on several placements can give you a useful variety of experience; at its worst it can be confusing and uncoordinated.

Guidelines for Working with Clients as a Counselling Student This is a checklist to help you to do this work in an appropriate way. (These notes are taken from guidelines on client work and training placements written by BAC for training agencies which apply for BAC recognition of their counsellor training course.[1] Not all courses are BAC-recognized, but BAC work to set standards for good practice and their guidelines give a useful marker for this.) I have added my own comments in italics after the relevant section.

- Evidence of clinical competence is an essential requirement for satisfactory completion of a BAC recognized course. The assessment of competence should be an integral part of the training and be carried out according to clear and specified criteria which are congruent with the core theoretical orientation of the course. *'Clinical competence', that is, the ability to work well with clients, must be practised and assessed. Gaining counselling experience under carefully monitored conditions is the only way to establish that a trainee can put what they learn into practice. Not everyone who can write an impressive theoretical paper can apply the theory in practice. Trainees need to know by what criteria their practice is to be assessed. If criteria are inappropriate, or worse, non-existent, a trainee is in danger of being assessed solely according to the personal preferences of the trainer(s).*

- There should be evidence that the student has established that he/she can provide and sustain contact with the client for the duration of the counselling contract. *It is all very well to acquire a repertoire of techniques, but they are only useful if they are applied in an appropriate way. Some clients need to settle down and establish a good measure of trust before they can get to the heart of the matter. If they are rushed they may 'make their excuses and leave'. Other clients need to feel that their counsellor can cope with whatever they throw at them. If they see a trainee who is anxious and hesitant they too may not stay the course. The well-being of the client must always come first.*

- The client work/counselling hours expected should be congruent with the theoretical orientation of the course; for example, a course that focuses on longer-term psychodynamic work would need to ask students for a larger number of hours in order to gain experience of working with a range of clients. *It may seem tough, but you need to have taken enough clients right through the counselling process if you are to show that you can do the job properly. In one year of trainee practice you may have four client sessions a week. If you see people for on average six sessions, by the end of the year you might easily have worked with over 20 clients. If you are doing open-ended work you may only have seen three or four people in the same time. It might be four or five years before you have had experience of working with 20 clients.*

- Limitations in the experience gained, e.g. restricted to young people, a particular setting etc. should be noted at the end of a course and needs for further experience and post-qualification training identi-fied. *This probably speaks for itself. I have talked elsewhere about the possibile difficulties of specializing too early.*

- All client work should be adequately supervised. *This cannot be repeated too often. It can be particularly useful when you start to see clients, to be in a supervision group with two or three trainees who are at a similar level of experience to you. In this situation you not only reflect on your own cases, but you also work with your fellow students on their work. This means that you learn from the practice of several people, not only your own.*

- Students have an obligation under the BAC Code of Ethics and Practice for Counsellors[2] to indicate their trainee status to an agency, and, if asked, to their clients. *Discuss! I agree absolutely with this guideline, but it is not easy to tell a client that you are a trainee in a way which does not raise their anxiety level. When a counsellor I know saw her first client as a trainee, the first words the client said to her were, 'I am very nervous, but I think that I will be all right, because I expect that you have a lot of experience, don't you?' What would you say if this happened to you?*

- Students (should) work according to the BAC Code of Ethics and Practice for Counsellors. The agency should also be working to this or a comparable code. *These codes are developed and scrutinized by experienced counselling practitioners. They provide a safe frame-work for you and your client. Make sure that you have a copy of the relevant code for your work and keep it where you can readily refer to it.*

- The desirability or otherwise of professional indemnity insurance for trainees should be considered. *Professional indemnity insurance protects you and your clients in case of injury to a client or claims against you of professional negligence.*

Here are some ways in which this work should not be done. (Extracts taken from BAC guidelines, as before.)

- Students should be working to specific *counselling* contracts, in whatever context, rather than exercising *counselling skills* within another context. *In other words, it is not appropriate to include as counselling practice activities such as talking to patients as you nurse them, or discussing career opportunities with sixth-formers in the course of teaching them, or helping a friend through a messy divorce.*

- It is not normally appropriate for students to take as clients other students on the course whether of their own or a different cohort. *Mixing roles causes confusion, whether it is students counselling other students, or trainers working on the course counselling students who they also teach, or someone supervising and counselling the same person; all are to be avoided.*

- It is not appropriate for inexperienced students in training to gain their client counselling experience through private/independent practice. (There may be exceptions to this last condition for students who are already experienced practitioners, but these exceptions will need to be carefully monitored.) *When you read the section in this chapter which covers independent practice, I think that you will see why it is not appropriate for a beginner. The same would be true of any other profession, and in many of them to work in this way would be illegal too. I once met someone who told me that he was a hypnotherapist. He had completed a six-week correspondence course in hypnotherapy and had set up in practice to help pay for further training. He advertised in the local paper and treated, he proudly told me, 'everything from giving up smoking to schizophrenia'. Would you have wanted to be treated by him? Of course, some counselling students are very experienced practitioners, who are 'topping up' their training. In this situation the trainers on the course will want to check that the student's independent practice conforms to the standards expected on the course.*

I am aware that all these conditions can seem quite alarming, so I want to end this section by wishing you well with your first clients. I promise you that you will remember them, probably because the work you do with them will be so fresh and exciting. There is some research which shows that counsellors are as effective, if not more effective, in the first six months of their work as they are when they are experienced practitioners. I would imagine that this is because they are working hard to understand what is happening, they are immersed in working on all aspects of counselling in their training, they are energized and enthusiastic, and they want to do well, for their sake as well as for their clients' sake.

Of course, there may be times when things do not run so smoothly. Clients may end counselling prematurely; they may be satisfied to make a small change when you feel that they could go much further. There are likely to be times when you feel clumsy or overwhelmed. Don't despair. That is why you have regular supervision and perhaps your own therapy to support you. In the end, you will probably find that you have learned as much, if not more, from the difficult times than the times when things run smoothly.

Working for an Agency under Supervision

One day, if you successfully get over all the assessment hurdles on your course, you will hold in your hand a diploma in counselling. Now you can begin to develop your career as a professional counsellor. At this point it is as well to remember the two kinds of professional practice recognized by the Counselling Register: agency practice and independent practice. As yet, this system is not statutory, but it has been set up with a lot of thought to best practice.

It is useful to look at how newly qualified members of other, more established professions start out on their professional careers, and apply some of these tried and tested career development paths to counselling. When doctors first qualify they are required to work for at least two years in hospitals, taking a gradually increasing amount of responsibility, under the watchful eye of senior practitioners. It is only after they have refined their skills in this way, to a standard which satisfies their consultants, that they are judged ready to take up a practice of their own. Teachers have a probationary year, during which they are assigned a senior teacher to be their mentor. This experienced practitioner observes some of the probationer's lessons and generally provides support and feedback.

Some training agencies divide the counselling qualifications they award into a first level, which is set at agency registration level, and an advanced level, which brings you to the standard required for independent practice. In order to obtain registration as an independent practitioner you must become a BAC accredited counsellor. You can only do this after you have had a full counsellor training and at least three years of counselling experience, completing 150 hours of counselling in each year. For all this work you are required to have supervision, presenting your cases to your supervisor for at least one and a half hours per month. Whether it is required of you as a condition of your training or not, the best way to start your professional counselling career is by working for a well-founded counselling agency.

Working as a Counsellor for a Counselling Agency A good counselling agency provides a working framework for the newly qualified counsellor just as a hospital provides for junior doctors. A good agency will give you all the services listed later in this chapter under 'The Basis for Good Practice'.

When you work for a counselling agency, the agency takes clinical responsibility for the counselling it provides. This means that responsibility for ensuring that your clients receive appropriate and efficient counselling is shared between you, your supervisor and the agency's counselling manager. When I worked for counselling agencies I often took this provision for granted, but when I started my own private practice I began to realize just how supportive it is to have others who share with you this weighty responsibility.

An agency also supplies you with clients. Well-established counselling organizations will be known in their area, by individuals who may seek counselling, and by individuals and organizations who will refer clients to them. At the counselling centre I helped to set up we 'wooed' the local GPs with invitations to join us for sessions of supper and information, all cunningly timed to start just after the end of evening surgery. I like to think that it was both the quality of the suppers and the counselling that we offered which persuaded them to refer many clients to us.

These are the tangible benefits of working for a counselling agency. There are many more which are less tangible. Do you remember the voluntary agency counsellor I interviewed? She talked about the sense of community, the feeling of a place where she could learn and grow, the sense of common purpose, and the way that the agency she worked for was concerned with people before bureaucracy. Counselling agencies, when they are working well, are concerned for the well-being not only of their clients, but also of their equally precious resources, their hard-working counsellors, supervisors, managers and administrators.

Working as a Counsellor in Independent Practice

If you are just beginning to think about embarking on counsellor training you may think that it is far too soon to consider the details of independent practice, but this work is the goal of most counselling trainees. It seems to me important at the start of your training to have a clear picture of what is involved in working independently. I hope that this section will convince you of the necessity of preparing carefully and thoroughly for this exacting work.

One bank holiday weekend we stayed with my stepson. He had recently qualified as a GP and on this bank holiday he was the duty doctor on call for the whole practice. It was a day which stretched his newly acquired abilities to the limit. For the first time it was his sole responsibility to diagnose his patients' ailments and prescribe the appropriate treatment. Every telephone call brought a new challenge. During the day he was called out to reassure the anxious parents of sick children, explain to patients the reason for the sudden onset of alarming symptoms, adjust treatment for a patient whose chronic illness had taken a turn for the worse; in other words, care for the unpredictable medical needs of the patients on his patch. It was an exciting and taxing time for him and for the rest of us, as we willed him on, knowing only the most general outline of the situations he faced, limited as he was in his accounts of what was happening by the requirements of professional confidentiality.

When you start out in independent practice you will face a similar time of excitement and stress. You too will be limited in sharing the details of your work by the need for professional confidentiality. Unlike my stepson, you also have to find your 'customers'. Many counsellors in independent practice work freelance, establishing a private counselling practice, and/or working for agencies which operate in a way which requires that their counsellors work autonomously. Some become involved in counselling-related activities such as teaching, supervision or management, in a counselling or counsellor training agency. Each kind of work has its special requirements.

At this point you should have reached the level of training and experience required for individual accreditation by BAC and be eligible for entry on the Register of Independent Practitioners. (I know that neither of these are statutory requirements, but you and your clients will be much more secure if you build your practice on this firm foundation.)

Independent practitioners with this level of qualification are equipped to undertake a wide range of work. Even if you are just embarking on counsellor training it will be useful for you to look forward to the goals for which you are preparing. Of course you may have a picture from the beginning of what you want to do and stick to it, but it is as well to know the range of options that might be open to you. My GP stepson talked during his training of the pros and cons of various medical specialisms and in the end made an informed choice to follow his first love, general practice.

Working for an Agency as an Independent Practitioner The two fastest growing sources of this work are: counselling as a member of a primary health care team for a general medical practice,[3] and counselling for an Employee Assistance Programme,[4] or a similar agency, which is contracted to provide counselling services for employees of organizations. The third widely available source of this kind of work is student counselling.[5] Working in these fields can provide interesting and varied experience, usually of brief, focused counselling.

Why does this work require you to be an independent practitioner? Agencies in this field are not primarily constituted as first-line counselling providers. It is true that Employee Assistance Programmes (EAPs) undertake to provide counselling to employees, but most of them then contract out the work to individual practitioners, working independently. In general practice, counsellors are members of the multi-disciplinary team, responsible for their own part of the general health service provided by the practice. In both cases the counsellor is expected to find for themselves most of the support services that would be provided for them in a counselling agency. Student counselling services usually work in a rather different way.

Most further education colleges and universities provide a counselling service as one aspect of the support services provided by their student services department. (Other related services offered through student services cover areas like housing, health, finance, etc.) There is usually more than one student counsellor and working conditions may be similar to those provided by a general counselling agency. The main difference is that most student counsellors have reached a level of training and experience appropriate for independent practitioners.

A few colleges and universities are contracting in independent counselling practitioners to give a fixed number of hours of counselling to their students. Counsellors working in this way of necessity carry more individual responsibility than members of student counselling teams. My personal view is that a student counsellor who is 'contracted in' is in a similar position to an agency nurse, or a locum doctor. All may work conscientiously, but they are unlikely to have the same in-depth knowledge of the place where they work, or the same commitment to the long-term welfare of their clients or patients.

Practitioners in each of these areas of work have formed specialized divisions within BAC. If you are thinking of working in any of these areas you would be well advised to contact the appropriate division through BAC. You will then have access to a network of information and contacts provided by experienced practitioners in the field. The relevant divisions are: Counselling in Medical Settings (CMS), the Association for Counselling at Work (ACW) and the Association for Student Counselling (ASC).

Working in Private Practice as an Independent Practitioner Many counselling trainees hope eventually to develop a counselling practice of their own. The advantages seem obvious – independence, status, higher earnings – but getting started is like setting up any other small business, with the same attendant risks. The 'newborn' private practitioner has to find a source of clients and suitable premises for their consulting room, find a supervisor, print stationery and do some careful financial calculations of the amount they need to find to pay the fixed costs involved in maintaining their practice. It is not long before dreams of earning enough to take holidays in the Caribbean begin to look more remote. There are particular points to consider if you are to establish a practice on a sound basis.

A Working Framework for Independent Practice Whether you work as an independent practitioner for an agency or in private practice, you need to provide for yourself and your clients all the professional support services to be found in a well-run counselling agency. This is where some significant aspects of your training can become very important. Training will have brought you into contact with many counselling practitioners. It is likely that they will form the basis of your professional network; people who you can turn to for support and further professional development. If your training agency has a graduate association it is a good idea to join it. If this is not possible you might think about forming informal associations with some of your fellow graduates. Finding some of the resources you need can be helped greatly by being part of a professional network.

Counselling-Related Work

Many independent counselling practitioners spend some of their time doing work other than seeing clients. The list below is not exhaustive, but covers the most common occupations in this field.

Trainer in Counselling Skills, Counselling and Counselling-Related Areas There is a wide range of work in this area, as this kind of training is undertaken by many people whose work uses counselling skills. In my work as a counselling skills trainer, I have taught people who work across a broad spectrum, including emergency service personnel, nurses and doctors, organizers of childminding services, bank staff, volunteer wardens for the elderly, as well as prospective counsellors embarking on the first stage of their training. In my experience this work can be fascinating, as long as you are prepared for the creative challenge of applying counselling skills to differing working situations.

Training counsellors is more focused work, in some ways, although it is a fallacy to suppose that teaching counselling skills is easier or more elementary. Students in either field quite rightly expect trainers to provide training which is professional and relevant. If you wish to work in this area you should consider fulfilling the necessary requirements to become a BAC-accredited counselling skills and/or counselling trainer.[6] If you are going to work in training you should also consider undertaking some training in teaching. Not everyone who is a good counsellor is good at teaching counselling.

Supervision As you know by now, all counsellors need a supervisor. Supervisors should be experienced counselling practitioners. Several counsellor training agencies also run training in supervision and BAC has an accreditation scheme for supervisors. If you prepare yourself in these ways supervision is very rewarding work.

Counselling and Training Management Every agency involved in the provision of counselling and counsellor training needs staff to manage this work. If you are a good organizer and enjoy working in a team this is another interesting field to consider. I have taken on many creative challenges in managing training provision over the years. It is very satisfying to establish successful training courses and watch them grow. It can also be nerve-racking, of course, when the students do not enrol and you have to make changes to cherished plans. You have to have something of an entrepreneurial spirit to enjoy this kind of work.

All of these activities are often undertaken by counselling practitioners working freelance. Counsellors are to be found working in the charitable, statutory and commercial sectors. Conditions and rates of pay vary enormously. When I began my independent practice a colleague told me that, in his experience, it could take five years to become fully established. There are probably more opportunities now than there were at that time, but you may at first need to travel long distances, or undertake work which is not very financially rewarding, in order to become established. It is all a great adventure, and you will need optimism, enthusiasm and perseverance to get you through the difficult times. Do it well, and your reward will be work which is endlessly fascinating and presents you each day with new creative challenges.

The Basis of Good Practice

Whether you are using counselling skills, counselling in an agency, or counselling in private practice, there are some issues which you need to think about, if you are to work safely and well. These points are mostly relevant to counsellors in general, but some refer to particular practice settings; for example private practice, or working for a counselling agency.

Confidentiality

If we are to be safely entrusted with the intimate details of someone's life, they need to be satisfied that their secrets are safe with us. When clients are asked what they value in counselling they frequently cite confidentiality as a major factor. Confidentiality is at the heart of good practice. There is no doubt that breaches in confidentiality are harmful to clients, and counsellors are very conscious of their responsibilities in this area. The consequence is that deliberate breaches are rare, but there are some situations in which the danger of leaks is increased. Every counselling practitioner, from the newest trainee to the most experienced supervisor, needs to guard against them.

Checklist of Confidentiality Risks

- Talking in the loo: there are times when we are offguard and sharing experiences with colleagues and friends. In these circumstances it is easy to let something slip. Even general comments can be problematic. For example, two students come out of a lecture on depression. One says to the other, 'I am not sure that I could cope with a depressed client. Imagine listening to all that doom and gloom week after week.' Nearby is a third person, who is, at that time, seeing a counsellor because she is depressed. She begins to wonder how her counsellor feels about her. Her depression deepens at the thought. She resolves to show a cheerful face to the counsellor next time that she sees her and to keep the worst of her depression to herself.

- 'Overlapping networks of confidential relationships':[7] this is a phrase used in the BAC *Code of Ethics and Practice for Counsellors* to describe the situation where, for instance, a counsellor talks to a supervisor, who then teaches a group of trainee counsellors, who then talk to each other. These professional networks are vital to provide support and training but it is important not to talk about clients in a way which could reveal their identity – for example, by referring to them by name or by divulging personal details about them – in these situations.

- 'Please will you see my friend': if a client is happy with his counsellor it is not surprising if he thinks of making her skills available to his friends and family. Any counsellor who is unwary enough to see the friend, or the partner, or the son or daughter, or any two clients with a close connection, soon becomes the repository of information about one person, told by the other person. In these circumstances it becomes impossible to remember who said what and maintaining confidentiality is a nightmare.

At the same time, if we are to do our work properly, we need to share some of the information which clients give us. In the course of training and practising it is important to discuss our work with a supervisor, and to write case studies, to show that we can make links between theory and practice. Some of us also write about counselling for publication in books and journals. It is important that knowledge is shared, so that we can learn from the experiences of others, not just from our own experience, and yet clients' interests must be protected. Sometimes these two necessities can seem incompatible.

Fortunately, many able and experienced counsellors have wrestled with this conundrum. The fruits of their deliberations are enshrined in various codes of ethics and practice. Here are some extracts on confidentiality from the BAC *Code of Ethics and Practice for Counsellors*. (The full code is reproduced in the Appendix.) I have used these extracts from the code to give you some ethical dilemmas to consider in relation to confidentiality. I have not supplied you with answers to the ethical dilemmas, because there is no answer that will fit every time one of these situations arises. When you are practising you will, of course, discuss each case with your supervisor, but it helps to think about some of the issues you may face. When you are thinking about issues of confidentiality, the first clause quoted from the *Code of Ethics and Practice for Counsellors* must always be kept in mind. The client's needs must come first. (The reference numbers – B.4.1 etc. – denote where the clause is to be found in the *Code*.)

> B.4.1 Confidentiality is a means of providing the client with safety and privacy. For this reason any limitation on the degree of confidentiality offered is likely to diminish the usefulness of counselling.

Now read this excerpt from the *Code* (clause B.4.4) and use it to help you to reflect on the ethical dilemma which follows.

> B.4.4 Exceptional circumstances may arise which give the counsellor good grounds for believing that the client will cause serious physical harm to others or themselves, or have harm caused to him/her. In such circumstances the client's consent to a change in the agreement about confidentiality should be sought whenever possible unless there are also good grounds

for believing the client is no longer able to take responsibility for his/her own actions. Whenever possible the decision to break confidentiality agreed between a counsellor and client should be made only after consultation with a counselling supervisor or an experienced counsellor.

Ethical Dilemma 1 You are seeing a client who tells you that her husband occasionally beats her up. She says that she has not tried to leave him because he said that wherever she went he would find her and kill her. She is getting more and more depressed and seems unable to do much to take care of herself. What aspects of this situation would lead you to seek her consent to a change in the agreement about confidentiality? How do you think she might react? If she refused, what would you do?

Here is another knotty ethical issue. Once again, read the section from the code (clause B.4.7) and use it to help you consider the dilemma which follows it.

B.4.7 If counsellors include consultations with colleagues and others within the confidential relationship, this should be stated to the client at the beginning of counselling.

Ethical Dilemma 2 A client says to you, 'I am going to tell you something that is very important to me but you must promise never to tell anyone else.' What would be your reply?

The third ethical issue I invite you to consider concerns suicide. Here the *Code of Ethics and Practice for Counsellors* acknowledges that counsellors' points of view about best practice will differ. This puts responsibility back on to you to consider your own position. Once again read the section of the code and reflect on the dilemma which follows.

B.4.11 Counsellors hold different views about whether or not a client expressing serious suicidal intentions forms sufficient grounds for breaking confidentiality. Counsellors should consider their own views and practice and communicate them to clients and any significant others where appropriate.

Ethical Dilemma 3 If a client expresses the intention to 'end it all' on the anniversary of her husband's death and tells you that she is hoarding the pills prescribed to her by her GP for that purpose, what would you take into account in deciding what to do? What is your position on suicide?

Do you believe that every attempt should be made to prevent it or do you feel that each person should be free to decide whether or not to go on living?

Ethical dilemmas as difficult as this are not common, but they do happen. I hope that I have not alarmed you too much by facing you with three of the most difficult situations one after the other. Let me end this section with something that you can use in every counselling session, not only when things are really difficult. My first supervisor said something about confidentiality which I have always remembered. 'When a client tells you a secret, they should be able to feel both that you now share the secret knowledge, and that it still belongs to them; that they have not lost it.' Like all the best teaching, this made immediate sense and still, twenty years on, I revisit it sometimes, and reflect again on what it might mean to have a secret which is shared and yet still belongs to me, and to share a secret and thereby lose it.

Before I end this section I should ask you to note that you are legally obliged to break confidentiality and inform the police in some circumstances related to the prevention of terrorism. Check the *Code of Ethics* clause B.5.1 for details.

Suitable Practical Resources

A client can be put off counselling before they have ever met their counsellor. Before they begin their first counselling session they will have obtained information about the help which they are about to receive, made an appointment, and entered the building where the counselling is to take place. It is important that what happens at all these points allays anxiety and inspires trust in the professional care of the counselling they are to receive.

Consulting Room Counselling is best done in a place which is private, quiet and discreet. It should not be obvious that clients are consulting a counsellor. This is particularly important if you live in a small community, where everyone knows what is going on. The counselling room should be suitably furnished with comfortable chairs, visible clocks and the essential large box of tissues, and equipped in a way which is comfortable, without being intimidating. It can be problematic, for example, to use a room which is too frilly and feminine, too smart or too shabby. I would question whether it is useful to have religious or political symbols about the place. Of course, if you are using counselling skills in the context of other work it is not always possible or desirable to meet all of these conditions; a nurse will usually talk with patients and relatives in a busy ward, most people who talk to a priest would expect to find religious symbols on the wall, and so on.

Waiting Room There should, where possible, be somewhere discreet where clients can wait for their session time. This is especially important if someone is being counselled in the same building in which they live and/or work. In colleges, for example, it is not appropriate to have the waiting area for the student counselling service in a place where it will be obvious to other students and staff that one of their number is seeing a counsellor.

Toilet Facilities They do not have to be elaborate, but they are necessary. Just think about the effect that strong feelings have on your metabolism.

Appointment and Message Facilities If you are fortunate there will be a receptionist or secretary to help with this. It is more likely that there will be an answering machine. There must be some way for clients and counsellors to send and receive confidential messages about appointments.

Secure Storage Facilities for Client Records It is vital to have the means to store client records and notes securely under lock and key. If records are kept on computer you need to find out about the Data Protection Act.[8] This is a law which regulates the storage of confidential information on computers.

Professional Support
Medical Back-up All counselling agencies should have a policy about communicating with doctors and other professionals who may be dealing with their clients. Some counsellors inform a client's GP that they are in counselling. I say to clients who come to me for open-ended counselling, 'Please let me have the name and address of your GP. I am asking for this to ensure that you have access to all the care you may need. I will write a letter to your GP to let them know that you are having counselling with me and asking them to tell me if there are any contraindications to you having this treatment. I will write again at the end of your counselling, simply to let them know that you are no longer having counselling. If I feel that it is important to be in touch with your doctor during your counselling I will discuss it with you, and only talk to them if I have your permission to do so.'

There have been occasions in my counselling career when it was important to be in touch with a client's doctor during their counselling. One of my clients suffered from a neurological disorder, for which treatment with powerful drugs was necessary. These drugs affected aspects of her moods and perception. Correspondence with the neurologist, done with the client's permission, was invaluable in helping me to know how to help the client to deal with the distorting effects of the drug treatment, and with the symptoms of the disease from which she suffered.

Dealing with an Emergency Counselling is inevitably at times a highly charged situation. Responsible counselling agencies take care to have help available for clients and counsellors in an emergency. In my experience, medical emergencies are rare, but clients with stress-related conditions such as asthma or some forms of heart disease may become physically distressed during their session. You should be prepared to deal with them. Threats of violence are extremely rare, but can be very frightening if you are alone. You need to learn how to 'talk down' someone from an agitated state and how to cope if you are threatened. Wherever possible there should be someone on hand to help out in an emergency. Some thought should be given to providing safety measures such as 'panic buttons' for counsellors who may need them.

Psychiatric Back-up Just as a client may need medical help, some may need psychiatric care. This may not be obvious when you start to work with them, but just as someone undergoing medical or surgical treatment runs a small risk of a severe reaction, counselling may bring to the surface deeper disturbances. If you work for a counselling agency, they should have a consultant psychiatrist, who will advise where appropriate. With experience your diagnostic skills will improve and the risks of accidentally provoking a serious disturbance should diminish from small to rare, but other factors – for example a traumatic upheaval in the client's life – can still upset the apple-cart. It is likely that as you become more experienced you will be ready to take on more difficult and complex work and this may increase the possibility of this kind of reaction. If eventually you set up in private practice you will need to ensure that you have psychiatric cover.

Professional Indemnity Insurance If you are working for an agency, check whether they provide you with this, or expect you to provide it for yourself. Counselling is a responsible job. It is rare for a counsellor to be sued by a client, but it does happen, and then legal costs can be high. Professional standards of practice help to minimize the risks, but nothing can eliminate them. There are also more practical considerations. If a client falls down some steps and breaks a leg they may claim compensation for the injury. BAC and other professional associations will put you in touch with insurance companies which will provide cover for personal injury and professional indemnity.

Continuing Professional Development Supervision alone is not enough. As the professionalization of counselling progresses, you will be increasingly expected to produce evidence of continued professional development. In any case, as your practice develops, you will want to keep your creative energy level high by moving into deeper levels of understanding. Counsellors are in the business of encouraging people to make the most of themselves. If we do not practise what we preach it will show in our work. Theoretical understanding and technical expertise are developing so rapidly in counselling, that if you do not keep in touch with new developments you will soon fall behind more recently trained practitioners. It is also important to stand back and reflect on your work. I imagine that we have all come across the doctor, or lawyer, or teacher who has a well-rehearsed response to every situation, but is clearly working on 'automatic pilot' and is hardly aware of your presence. This is not good practice in any profession.

A Well-Organized Structure of Service Provision
A Sufficient Supply of Suitable Clients When you work for an agency you are provided with clients. When you work in private practice you have to build up your own referral network. You need to be prepared for the likelihood that it will take a while to build up a practice. This process is a bit like setting up a small business. First you have to establish a 'market'. You need to find sources of referrals of suitable clients. Some common sources are:

- an entry in a referral directory (the best known is the *Counselling and Psychotherapy Resources Directory* published by BAC)
- making contact with GPs in your area, letting them know about your practice
- some counsellor training agencies, which are also providers of counselling, maintain a referral-out system, passing on some of the clients who come to them for counselling to their graduates
- joining with other counsellors to form a referral network, which you advertise in your local area
- advertising in newspapers and magazines. Think carefully before you do this, especially if you work from home. Prospective clients may answer such advertisements for many reasons besides a wish to have counselling. Perhaps this is particularly so if the counsellor is a woman.

Once you have become known as reliable it will become easier to maintain your practice and fill any spaces in your schedule quickly. When you calculate the income you need to keep body and soul together bear in mind that, if private practice is your main source of income, you are not paid for your holidays, or when you are ill, and even the most efficient and well-known counsellor will not fill all the spaces in their practice immediately. You need to take all these factors into account and make the necessary provision for them when you make your financial calculations, if you are not to encounter cash flow problems.

An Intake Assessment System When you work for a counselling agency, new clients are usually assessed by specially trained intake counsellors. In private practice you have to do this assessment yourself. Before you set up in private practice you should seriously consider training in the specialized skills of intake and assessment. When such assessment is done well it can help to ensure that you only take on clients who have a good chance of benefiting from your help.

Good Case Management There are many practical considerations in providing clients with an efficient, well-run service. Thought must be given to:

- Fee Payment. Should a set fee be charged to all, or a sliding scale offered depending on the client's income? Should clients be asked to give a donation, or have to pay up front?
- Policy on Absences. Will all absences be charged for, or only those for which no notice was given? Are there guidelines about notification of absence from a session?
- Information for Clients about services provided and what to do if they wish to complain about the services they are given. It is important to give written information about the counselling service to clients, so that this can be easily referred to when necessary.
- A Code of Ethics and Practice. This helps to ensure high practice standards.
- Secure Record-Keeping Systems. It is not easy to design a system which is practicable, accessible and secure. If you have to carry notes around, make sure that they do not contain details which could reveal the identity of the client. When not in use, information must be kept under lock and key.
- A Counselling Contract, which should be made with clients, either verbally, or in writing, setting out the conditions under which the counselling is offered. The main areas covered by the contract are likely to be: expectations about attendance and policy on missed sessions and holiday breaks; the fee to be paid; the approach to be used; whether counselling is fixed-term or open-ended; the length

of notice to be given by either party before ending the contract; the code of ethics by which the counsellor practises; and a complaints procedure for the client to follow if they are not satisfied with the service they receive from their counsellor.

- A 'Therapeutic Executor'. In one counselling agency where I worked we used to refer to this amongst ourselves as the 'falling under a bus' provision. If you were to die suddenly, or meet with an accident, or in any way be unable to maintain your practice, what would happen to your clients? There have been several times in my career when I have worked with clients whose counsellors have become unavailable without warning. Sometimes this situation has been temporary, sometimes permanent. As you can imagine, this is a distressing situation for the clients concerned. It helps if there is a system already in place to ensure that they can see another counsellor as soon as possible, should they wish to. In a counselling agency, the counselling manager is responsible for this provision; in private practice you should ask another counsellor who uses the same counselling approach as you to hold a list of your current clients, and undertake to care for them in an emergency. Of course it is important to update this list regularly. You should then ensure that this 'therapeutic executor's' name and contact information is known to your family and to your supervisor, so that they can easily contact them.

Supervision

I have mentioned several times the importance of regular supervision. The confidential nature of a counsellor's work can place heavy burdens on her. For this and other reasons regular supervision is vital. Here is an extract from the BAC *Information Sheet on Supervision*.[9] It is the section headed 'Why supervision is essential for the practising counsellor'.

By its very nature, counselling makes considerable demands upon counsellors who may become overwhelmed, ignore some important point, become confused as to what is taking place within a particular client, or have undermining doubts about their own usefulness. It is difficult, if not sometimes impossible, to be objective about one's counselling and the opportunity to discuss it in confidence with a suitable person is invaluable. Good counselling also requires the counsellor to relate practice to theory and theory to practice. Supervision can help the counsellor to evolve practice and in this sense is one aspect of continuing training.

Through the supervision process the supervisor can ensure that the counsellor is addressing the needs of the client, can monitor the relationship between the counsellor and client to maximize the therapeutic effectiveness of the relationship and ensure that ethical standards are adhered to throughout the counselling process. Though not concerned primarily with training, personal therapy, or line management, supervisors will encourage and facilitate the ongoing self development, continued learning and self monitoring of the counsellor.

That is the theory, but how do a counsellor and supervisor work together? What kind of relationship does a counsellor have with their supervisor? This depends primarily on two factors: the level of experience reached by the counsellor and the counselling approach they use.

Supervision and Counselling Approaches As you read Chapter 6 on approaches, I hope that you got a sense of differences in the prime focus of the counsellor-client relationship in each approach. These differences will be reflected in supervision. The supervisor of a 'person-centred' counsellor, for example, will focus on whether and how the counsellor maintains qualities of empathy, genuineness and respect in relationships with their clients, and could be expected to maintain such a relationship herself in supervision sessions. Such a supervisor is likely to be facilitative, rather than didactic. Behavioural and cognitive counselling methods have a much stronger element of 're-education'. Supervision for these approaches is likely to focus on the behaviour of the client and the techniques used by the counsellor. The style of the supervisor is likely to be more didactic. In psychodynamic counselling the focus of the counsellor's work is to help the client to uncover and gain insight into unconscious dynamics, by observing and experiencing their manifestations in the content and process of the session, and in the development of the counsellor-client relationship.

To give an example: a counsellor talks to his supervisor about a client who dismisses the counsellor's responses. The counsellor feels that everything he says is useless, and he begins to feel both helpless and angry. Counsellor and supervisor look at why this might be happening. They use their knowledge of the client's past to give them clues; perhaps the client's parents ignored what she said to them, and this aspect is colouring her expectations of the counsellor. Sometimes a similar process will then happen in the supervision session and the counsellor will become unable to take in and use the supervisor's comments. The supervisor will point this out and then counsellor and supervisor will look at what is happening between them, as well as between the counsellor and his client. It is as if these currents of feeling are 'contagious'. Once the supervisor and counsellor recognize the pattern of feelings they can consider ways to help the client to become able to look at what might prevent her from taking in what is said to her, and from believing that the counsellor takes in and values what she has to say.

Supervision and the Counsellor's Level of Experience Trainee counsellors and newly qualified counsellors still need a considerable element of 'coaching' from their supervisor. The first time they face a particular counselling situation they will need to go through in detail ways that they might deal with it. When I supervise groups of trainees, who are starting to work with their first clients, we are likely to spend some time revising first principles: how to make contact with a client for the first time (Is it best to write or telephone? What do you do if a member of the client's family answers the telephone, and asks who you are? . . . and so on); how to keep appropriate records; and how to deal with the first session. However well a counsellor is trained, there is nothing like coming face-to-face with your first clients to make you really think in detail about what you are doing.

After practising for a time counsellors will become ready to take the reins more into their own hands. At this point it is important that they are enabled to move from 'counselling by the book' to developing their own distinctive style. It is like taking away your supporting hand from the saddle of a child's bicycle and encouraging him to ride by himself. At first there may be some alarming wobbles. It is the supervisor's task at this stage to foster the counsellor's independence and to try to ensure that the counsellor proceeds when she is ready, so that neither the clients nor the counsellor are injured in the process. As a supervisor I find this an especially interesting stage, and a creative challenge. The client's needs are paramount, as they are in all supervision, but each of the counsellors who I supervise works in a different way, and has their own strengths and weaknesses. One is good at objective analysis, but stays a bit aloof, and needs help to be fully emotionally engaged; another is acutely sensitive to the flow of feelings in the session, but finds it hard to step back and make sense of them. The baseline is that they should all be working with integrity, efficiency and appropriate care.

Finally, a counsellor with a good deal of experience may not see their supervisor so frequently (once a week is usual at first; BAC requires all its practitioner members, even those who have reached accreditation level, to have supervision for at least one and a half hours per month). An experienced counsellor uses her supervisor as a colleague, who she consults about the progress of her cases. She may not talk about all her clients, or may mention some only infrequently. She is likely to talk about the tight corners in her work and to use her supervisor as a 'sounding board' for her thought on how to deal with them.

Here is an experienced counsellor talking with her supervisor about a case referred to her for brief counselling in the health centre where she works. (*C* = counsellor and *S* = supervisor)

> C I saw X for his first session. He has consulted the doctor several times in the past year. Each time he has complained of different symptoms: backache, persistent sore throat, stomach upsets. The doctor has given him medication and a 'sick note'. He has taken a short time off work and the symptoms have eased. He has a responsible job. Last time he saw the doctor he talked about feeling stressed and the doctor suggested counselling. He came because he trusts the doctor, but he is a bit wary. It was clear in the first session that he is under a lot of stress and is waking up in the night with what sounds from his description like panic attacks, although he is afraid that the symptoms might be signs of heart trouble. I feel that he really needs some long-term counselling, but when I suggested that we talk about the possibility he made it quite clear that he had agreed to six sessions of counselling and that was it. 'I am a busy man,' he said. I am not sure where to go from here.

> S Well, it seems like a good idea at this point for us to look at what your options are and at how you might make a start at finding a focus for your work with X.

Counsellor and supervisor will work together on this, looking at how the counsellor might proceed in the limited time that she has with her client. This kind of reflection has a particular kind of value in brief work, when there is not time for the counsellor to wait to see what emerges with the client over time. In this case they are likely to review the coping skills that the client has, and the counsellor will encourage him to use them to help himself. If he finds that the counselling helps he may be encouraged to take it further at some point.

Forms of Supervision A counsellor may see her supervisor individually, or may be a member of a supervision group of up to four counsellors, working with one supervisor. Some counsellors seek out others who have reached a similar level of experience and form a peer group for supervision. (This method is more appropriate for experienced counsellors than beginners.)

Remember the counsellors talking about their work in Chapter 2? They talked about the importance to them of supervision. I have remembered, as I worked on this section, the times I have been grateful for the support, and clear-sightedness of my various supervisors: the time a client threatened to commit suicide; the times a session touched a sore spot in me and left me feeling useless, or hurt, or furious or even shocked and traumatized. Each of my many supervisors has helped me to see my work from a different perspective and bring new insight to it. After twenty years of practice I would not want to work without them.

Postscript

All this detail about supervision can leave you feeling as if you have a bossy parent at your shoulder, who is always asking you if you have tidied your room, when you want to close the door and get on with the work itself, but I believe that, if we get these conditions right, then we and our clients have the basis for our work together. The picture I have of the way this is done comes from the work of Donald Winnicott.[10]

Dr Winnicott was a paediatrician who became a psychoanalyst specializing in the analysis of children. He described the way that a good mother creates a safe space for her child. She ensures that the child cannot come to any harm, that he has all that he needs, and because she takes care of this framework, the child is free to explore, to try things out, to play with ideas and to test them out. That is what our detailed preparations are designed to produce: a space in which our clients can explore in safety, because they can be sure that we have prepared it with their needs in mind.

9
From the Counsellor's Chair

I sit in my chair in my consulting room reflecting on my experience of being a counsellor. I vividly remember the first session of the first counselling skills I attended. Like the rest of the group I introduced myself and said that I had come on the course because I wanted to help people and do some good in the world. At some point in that session the trainer asked us how we felt when someone confided in us about a painful and difficult aspect of their life. As the discussion began I searched my mind for the 'right' answer. I thought of the times when someone had shared a painful secret with me. How did I feel? Ambivalent. On one hand I felt privileged to be entrusted with something so precious and personal; on the other hand I felt apprehensive, burdened, sometimes resentful, about the weight of painful knowledge which I too now held. I did not know what to do with this knowledge. Was I expected to take responsibility for it? Was it my job to solve these weighty problems and make the person happy again? What if they came to rely on my support and stayed dependent on me for ever? What if their trust in me was misplaced, and I was not the strong and reliable person that they imagined me to be? (By this time, with so many doubts in my mind, this last seemed to be a racing certainty.)

Then the trainer turned to me. 'What do you think, Val?' Now what was I to do? Fix a confident smile on my face and act as if I sorted out six intractable problems before breakfast each day? Or own up to all this doubt? I decided that I would not be able to keep up the confident act, so I shared my confusion. I was amazed to discover that there was not a 'right answer' to the question the trainer had posed; rather that we were all invited to acknowledge our responses and try to understand them. Each person's contribution was valued and considered. This was not like my previous experiences of training. We were not to be 'force fed' with information. A student on a counselling course I taught later put it more succinctly. In answer to the question, 'What have you most valued about the course?' he said, 'I came looking for answers to my questions. I have not been given many answers, but the questions have got more interesting.' Of course my experience of training was not all sweetness and light. There were times when it stirred up painful memories, or I made a mess of a role-play and felt foolish and inept, but from that first session I was hooked and twenty years on the questions are still getting more interesting.

I remember too the experience of embarking on my own therapy. What an enormous and risky step it was to entrust a stranger with my secrets. There were times when it felt like torture. I was sure that my counsellor had the answers to the problems I brought, and I did not understand why he could not or would not tell me what they were. It was a while before I understood the importance of patiently uncovering my own insights.

Sitting in the counsellor's chair has not been as I imagined it would be when I began. I thought that I would learn 'how to do it', and of course I have developed knowledge and experience of what to do, but I did not realize that how *I* am would be so important. I thought right at the beginning that I would be expected to provide my clients with answers, but I discovered that I have to help them to find their own. My task is to work with them to prepare the ground, so that the answers can emerge. It is a bit like two people setting out to cultivate a neglected garden together. One may have had more experience of gardening, but the garden belongs to the other, and must meet their needs if it is to give them pleasure and satisfaction. Both share the pleasure when a knotty piece of undergrowth is cleared, and a glorious flower emerges, and both share the pain and disappointment when a treasured plant fails to thrive. At the end of their work the counsellor gardener leaves and the client gardener continues to cultivate the garden alone, using the understanding acquired along the way.

If you become a counsellor now you join us at an exciting time. The pioneering days when I began had their own excitements, of course, but those days are over. As you have discovered in the course of reading this book, counsellors are everywhere, or nearly everywhere. You are likely to have more work opportunities available to you than there were when I began. You will also need to be prepared to be under more public scrutiny. As counselling has come of age and become more influential, it is inevitable that there has been a corresponding increase in public concern. There has also been a cultural shift in attitudes to professional care during that time. The days are over when 'experts' and professionals were treated with deference. When a doctor prescribes treatment for our ills, most of us expect to be able to question her and to be given information about the effects of the treatment. We want to know why teachers use particular methods of teaching, and we expect to be able to choose to send our children to a school which suits us and them. If something goes wrong with the professional care we receive, we expect to be able to complain, to have our complaint investigated, and to be given an explanation, and even compensation, if the investigation finds that we have not been well cared for.

With public concern comes media attention. It would be a poor journalist who did not keep abreast of the issues of the day. Media criticisms of counselling and counsellors fall into two categories. One argument is that we are too powerful. Fears are voiced that we will take over and insist that counselling should be compulsory in some situations. These critics report the cases of people who feel that counselling has harmed them, has put ideas into their head, has damaged their relationships. It is a terrifying thought that we might seek help for pain and distress and face the possibility of emerging in a worse state than ever. It is the fear we often take with us when we have to go into hospital, or take powerful medication. When I see accounts of these cases I sorrow for the hurt of the people concerned and I think of all my colleagues who work to improve standards of counselling care. Their work, of course, is not news.

The other criticism counsellors face in the media is that we are accused of having no useful expertise, of doing work which is based on theories which are said to be unproven, and of using methods the efficacy of which has not been subject to scientific scrutiny. This is always a difficult criticism to counter, particularly when 'cure' is seen as the measure of successful treatment, and the goals of improved quality of life and a greater sense of well-being are regarded as private concerns, as a doctor argued recently in the press. There is research evidence which can be cited on both sides of this debate. I can only say that I do not think that I and my clients and the students I have taught have been wasting our time and money over the last 20 years, but you will have to find out for yourself whether you feel the same.

Counsellors have to work in this climate. Most of us, most of the time, welcome the discipline which public accountability brings, but our work can be risky, and such scrutiny highlights the risks. If I am faced with a client who is haunted by nightmares which may arise from almost inaccessible memories of having been sexually abused as a child, or may be fantasy images, springing from their own unconscious (no less real than memories of course), do I agree to work with them? Or am I scared off by the newspaper stories about counsellors producing 'false memory syndrome', convincing a client that they were abused, when no abuse occurred? If a client is suicidal, do I take them on, and face the possible anguish and anger of their family, not to mention my own distress and sense of helplessness, if the client does commit suicide? Usually, of course, if I feel that I have the skills to work with them, I do take them on. A counsellor, like a doctor, would not get very far if they did not treat the patient for fear that they might not recover, or might experience some pain during treatment, but I am grateful for the professional support of my supervisor and of BAC, my professional association, at such times.

Counselling is a new profession. The medical profession had hundreds of years to get its act together. Nursing, social work and teaching all progressed slowly to regulation and clearly defined systems of qualification. We have gone through the same process in 20 years. It is not yet complete, but it is moving very fast. Who knows where counselling will be in 20 years' time? If you like a challenge and want to play your part in ensuring that high quality counselling is available to all who need it, then I hope that, like me, you will answer 'Yes' to the question:

Is counselling training for you?

Appendix

The British Association for Counselling Code of Ethics and Practice for Counsellors, May 1996

1. Status of this code

1.1 In response to the experience of members of BAC, this code is a revision of the 1992 code.

2. Introduction

2.1 The purpose of this code is to establish and maintain standards for counsellors who are members of BAC, and to inform and protect members of the public seeking and using their services.

2.2 All members of this Association are required to abide by existing codes appropriate to them. They thereby accept a common frame of reference within which to manage their responsibilities to clients, colleagues, members of this Association and the wider community. Whilst this code cannot resolve all ethical and practice related issues, it aims to provide a framework for addressing ethical issues and to encourage optimum levels of practice. Counsellors will need to judge which parts of this code apply to particular situations. They may have to decide between conflicting responsibilities.

2.3 This Association has a Complaints Procedure which can lead to the expulsion of members for breaches of its Codes of Ethics and Practice.

3. The Nature of Counselling

3.1 The overall aim of counselling is to provide an opportunity for the client to work towards living in a more satisfying and resourceful way. The term 'counselling' includes work with individuals, pairs or groups of people often, but not always, referred to as 'clients'. The objectives of particular counselling relationships will vary according to the clients' needs. Counselling may be concerned with developmental issues, addressing and resolving specific problems, making decisions, coping with crisis, developing personal insight and knowledge, working through feelings of inner conflict or improving relationships with others. The counsellor's role is to facilitate the client's work in ways which respect the client's values, personal resources and capacity for self-determination.

3.2 Only when both the user and the recipient explicitly agree to enter into a counselling relationship does it become 'counselling' rather than the use of 'counselling skills'.

3.3 It is not possible to make a generally accepted distinction between counselling and psychotherapy. There are well founded traditions which use the terms interchangeably and others which distinguish them. Regardless of the theoretical approaches preferred by individual counsellors, there are ethical issues which are common to all counselling situations.

4. *The Structure of this Code*

This code has been divided into two parts. The Code of Ethics outlines the fundamental values of counselling and a number of general principles arising from these. The Code of Practice applies these principles to the counselling situation.

A. *Code of Ethics*

A.1 Counselling is a non-exploitative activity. Its basic values are integrity, impartiality, and respect. Counsellors should take the same degree of care to work ethically whether counselling is paid or voluntary.

A.2 *Client Safety:*

All reasonable steps should be taken to ensure the client's safety during counselling.

A.3 *Clear Contracts:*

The terms on which counselling is being offered should be made clear to clients before counselling commences. Subsequent revisions of these terms should be agreed in advance of any change.

A.4 *Competence:*

Counsellors shall take all reasonable steps to monitor and develop their own competence and to work within the limits of that competence. This includes having appropriate and ongoing counselling supervision/ consultative support.

B. *Code of Practice*
B.1 *Introduction:*

This code applies these values and ethical principles to more specific situations which may arise in the practice of counselling.

B.2 *Issues of Responsibility:*

B.2.1 The counsellor-client relationship is the foremost ethical concern, but it does not exist in social isolation. For this reason, the counsellor's responsibilities to the client, to themselves, colleagues, other members of the Association and members of the wider community are listed under separate headings.

B.2.2 To the Client:

Client Safety
2.2.1 Counsellors should take all reasonable steps to ensure that the client suffers neither physical nor psychological harm during counselling.

2.2.2 Counsellors do not normally give advice.

Client Autonomy
2.2.3 Counsellors are responsible for working in ways which promote the client's control over his/her own life, and respects the client's ability to make decisions and change in the light of his/her own beliefs and values.

2.2.4 Counsellors do not normally act on behalf of their clients. If they do, it will be only at the express request of the client, or else in the exceptional circumstances detailed in B.4.

2.2.5 Counsellors are responsible for setting and monitoring boundaries between the counselling relationship and any other kind of relationship, and making this explicit to the client.

2.2.6 Counsellors must not exploit their clients financially, sexually, emotionally, or in any other way. Engaging in sexual activity with the client is unethical.

2.2.7 Clients should be offered privacy for counselling sessions. The client should not be observed by anyone other than their counsellor(s) without having given his/her informed consent. This also applies to audio/video taping of counselling sessions.

Pre-Counselling Information
2.2.8 Any publicity material and all written and oral information should reflect accurately the nature of the service on offer, and the training, qualifications and relevant experience of the counsellor (see also B.6).

2.2.9 Counsellors should take all reasonable steps to honour undertakings offered in their pre-counselling information.

Contracting
2.2.10 Clear contracting enhances and shows respect for the client's autonomy.

2.2.11 Counsellors are responsible for communicating the terms on which counselling is being offered, including availability, the degree of confidentiality offered, and their expectations of clients regarding fees, cancelled appointments and any other significant matters. The communication of terms and any negotiations over these should be concluded before the client incurs any financial liability.

2.2.12 It is the client's choice whether or not to participate in counselling. Reasonable steps should be taken in the course of the counselling relationship to ensure that the client is given an opportunity to review the terms on which counselling is being offered and the methods of counselling being used.

2.2.13 Counsellors should avoid unnecessary conflicts of interest and are expected to make explicit to the client any relevant conflicts of interest.

2.2.14 If records of counselling sessions are kept, clients should be made aware of this. At the client's request information should be given about access to these records, their availability to other people, and the degree of security with which they are kept (see B.4).

2.2.15 Counsellors have a responsibility to establish with clients what other therapeutic or helping relationships are current. Counsellors should gain the client's permission before conferring with other professional workers.

2.2.16 Counsellors should be aware that computer-based records are subject to statutory regulations under the Data Protection Act 1984. From time to time the government introduces changes in the regulations concerning the client's right of access to his/her own records. Current regulations have implications for counsellors working in social service and health care settings.

Counsellor Competence

2.2.17 Counsellors should monitor actively the limitations of their own competence through counselling supervision/consultative support, and by seeking the views of their clients and other counsellors. Counsellors should work within their own known limits.

2.2.18 Counsellors should not counsel when their functioning is impaired due to personal or emotional difficulties, illness, disability, alcohol, drugs or for any other reason.

2.2.19 It is an indication of the competence of counsellors when they recognise their inability to counsel a client or clients and make appropriate referrals.

B.2.3 To Former Clients:

2.3.1. Counsellors remain accountable for relationships with former clients and must exercise caution over entering into friendships, business relationships, sexual relationships, training and other relationships. Any changes in relationship must be discussed in counselling supervision. The decision about any change(s) in relationship with former clients should be taken into account whether the issues and power dynamics present during the counselling relationship have been resolved and properly ended.

2.3.2. Counsellors who belong to organisations which prohibit sex with all former clients are bound by that commitment.

B.2.4 To Self as Counsellor:

2.4.1. Counsellors have a responsibility to themselves and their clients to maintain their own effectiveness, resilience and ability to help clients. They are expected to monitor their own personal functioning and to seek help and/or withdraw from counselling, whether temporarily or permanently, when their personal resources are sufficiently depleted to require this (see also B.3).

2.4.2 Counsellors should have received adequate basic training before commencing counselling, and should maintain ongoing professional development.

2.4.3 Counsellors are encouraged to review periodically their need for professional indemnity insurance and to take out such a policy when appropriate.

2.4.4 Counsellors should take all reasonable steps to ensure their own physical safety.

B.2.5 To other Counsellors:

2.5.1 Counsellors should not conduct themselves in their counselling-related activities in ways which undermine public confidence in either their role as a counsellor or in the work of other counsellors.

2.5.2 If a counsellor suspects misconduct by another counsellor which cannot be resolved or remedied after discussion with the counsellor concerned, they should implement the Complaints Procedure, doing so without breaches of confidentiality other than those necessary for investigating the complaint (see B.9).

B.2.6 To Colleagues and Members of the Caring Professions:

2.6.1 Counsellors should be accountable for their services to colleagues, employers and funding bodies as appropriate. The means of achieving this should be consistent with respecting the needs of the client outlined in B.2.2.7, B.2.2.13 and B.4.

2.6.2 Counsellors are encouraged to increase their colleagues' understanding of the counselling role. No colleague or significant member of the caring professions should be led to believe that a service is being offered by the counsellor which is not, as this may deprive the client of the offer of such a service from elsewhere.

2.6.3 Counsellors should accept their part in exploring and resolving conflicts of interest between themselves and their agencies, especially where this has implications for the client (see also B.2.213).

B.2.7 To the Wider Community:

Law
2.7.1 Counsellors should work within the law.
2.7.2 Counsellors should take all reasonable steps to be aware of current law affecting the work of the counsellor. A counsellor's ignorance of the law is no defence against legal liability or penalty including inciting or 'counselling', which has a specific legal sense, the commission of offences by clients.

Social Context
2.7.3 Counsellors will take all reasonable steps to take account of the client's social context.

B.3 Counselling Supervision/Consultative Support:

B.3.1 It is a breach of the ethical requirement for counsellors to practise without regular counselling supervision/consultative support.
B.3.2 Counselling supervision/consultative support refers to a formal arrangement which enables counsellors to discuss their counselling regularly with one or more people who have an understanding of counselling and counselling supervision/consultative support. Its purpose is to ensure the efficacy of the counsellor-client relationship. It is a confidential relationship (see also B.4).
B3.3 Counsellors who have line managers owe them appropriate managerial accountability for their work. The counselling supervisor role should be independent of the line manager role. However where the counselling supervisor is also the line manager, the counsellor should also have access to independent consultative support.
B.3.4 The volume of supervision should be in proportion to the volume of counselling work undertaken and the experience of the counsellor.
B.3.5 Whenever possible, the discussion of cases within supervision/consultative support should take place without revealing the personal identity of the client.
B.3.6 The ethics and practice of counselling supervision/consultative support are outlined further in their own specific code: the Code of Ethics and Practice for the Supervision of Counsellors (see also B.9).

B.4 Confidentiality: Clients, Colleagues and Others:

B.4.1 Confidentiality is a means of providing the client with safety and privacy. For this reason any limitation on the degree of confidentiality offered is likely to diminish the usefulness of counselling.

B.4.2 Counsellors treat with confidence personal information about clients, whether obtained directly or indirectly or by inference. Such information includes name, address, biographical details, and other descriptions of the client's life and circumstances which might result in identification of the client.

B.4.3 Counsellors should work within the current agreement with their client about confidentiality.

B.4.4 Exceptional circumstances may arise which give the counsellor good grounds for believing that the client will cause serious physical harm to others or themselves, or have harm caused to him/her. In such circumstances the client's consent to a change in the agreement about confidentiality should be sought whenever possible unless there are also good grounds for believing the client is no longer able to take responsibility for his/her own actions. Whenever possible, the decision to break confidentiality agreed between a counsellor and client should be made only after consultation with a counselling supervisor or an experienced counsellor.

B.4.5 Any breaking of confidentiality should be minimised both by restricting the information conveyed to that which is pertinent to the immediate situation and to those persons who can provide the help required by the client. The ethical considerations involve balancing between acting in the best interests of the client and in ways which enable clients to resume taking responsibility for their actions, a very high priority for counsellors, and the counsellor's responsibilities to the wider community (see B.2.7 and B.4.4).

B.4.6 Counsellors should take all reasonable steps to communicate clearly the extent of the confidentiality they are offering to clients. This should normally be made clear in the pre-counselling information or initial contracting.

B.4.7 If counsellors include consultations with colleagues and others within the confidential relationship, this should be stated to the client at the beginning of counselling.

B.4.8 Care must be taken to ensure that personally identifiable information is not transmitted through overlapping networks of confidential relationships. For this reason, it is good practice to avoid identifying specific clients during counselling supervision/consultative support and other consultations, unless there are sound reasons for doing so (see also B.2.2.14 and B.4.2).

B.4.9 Any agreement between the counsellor and client about confidentiality may be reviewed and changed by joint negotiations.

B.4.10 Agreements about confidentiality continue after the client's death unless there are overriding legal or ethical considerations.

B.4.11 Counsellors hold different views about whether or not a client expressing serious suicidal intentions forms sufficient grounds for breaking confidentiality. Counsellors should consider their own views and practice and communicate them to clients and any significant others where appropriate (see also B.2.6.2).

B.4.12 Special care is required when writing about specific counselling situations for case studies, reports or publication. It is important that the author either has the client's informed consent, or effectively disguises the client's identity.

B.4.13 Any discussion between the counsellor and others should be purposeful and not trivialising.

B.5 Confidentiality in the Legal Process:

B.5.1 Generally speaking, there is no legal duty to give information spontaneously or on request until instructed to do so by a court. Refusal to answer police questions is not an offence, although lying could be. In general terms, the only circumstances in which the police can require an answer about a client, and when refusal to answer would be an offence, relate to the prevention of terrorism. It is good practice to ask police personnel to clarify their legal right to an answer before refusing to give one.

B.5.2 Withholding information about a crime that one knows has been committed or is about to be committed is not an offence, save exceptionally. Anyone hearing of terrorist activities should immediately take legal advice.

B.5.3 There is no legal obligation to answer a solicitor's enquiry or to make a statement for the purpose of legal proceedings, unless ordered to do so by a court.

B.5.4 There is no legal obligation to attend court at the request of parties involved in a case, or at the request of their lawyers, until a witness summons or subpoena is issued to require attendance to answer questions or produce documents.

B.5.5 Once in the witness box, there is a duty to answer questions when instructed to do so by the court. Refusal to answer could be punished as contempt of court unless there are legal grounds for not doing so. (It has been held that communications between the counsellor and client during an attempt at 'reconciliation' in matrimonial cases are privileged and thus do not require disclosure unless the client waives this privilege. This does not seem to apply to other kinds of cases.)

B.5.6 The police have powers to seize confidential files if they have obtained a warrant from a circuit judge. Obstructing the police from taking them in these circumstances may be an offence.

B.5.7 Counsellors should seek legal advice and/or contact this association if they are in any doubt about their legal rights and obligations before acting in ways which conflict with their agreement with clients who are directly affected (see also B.2.7.1).

B.6 Advertising/Public Statements:

B.6.1 When announcing counselling services, counsellors should limit the information to name, relevant qualifications, address, telephone number, hours available, and a brief listing of the services offered.

B.6.2 All such announcements should be accurate in every particular.

B.6.3 Counsellors should distinguish between membership of this Association and accredited practitioner status in their public statement. In particular, the former should not be used to imply the latter.

B.6.4 Counsellors should not display an affiliation with an organisation in a manner which falsely implies the sponsorship or verification of that organisation.

Directive made by the Management Committee 23 March 1996
Membership of BAC is not allowed to be mentioned by any person or organisation in press advertisements, in telephone directories, on business cards, on letterheads, on brass plates, on plaques, etc. BAC members are encouraged to make oral and written statements to the public and potential clients in letters and pre-counselling leaflets. These statements must include the fact that membership of BAC is not a qualification in counselling but means that the individual, and where appropriate the organisation, abides by the Codes of Ethics and Practice and is subject to the Complaints Procedure of the British Association for Counselling. Copies of the Codes and the Complaints Procedure are available from BAC.

This directive does not apply to BAC Recognised Courses, BAC Accredited Counsellors, Supervisors, Trainers and Fellows who receive separate instruction.

B.7 Research:

B.7.1 The use of personally identifiable material gained from clients or by the observation of counselling should be used only after the client has given consent, usually in writing, and care has been taken to ensure that consent was given freely.

B.7.2 Counsellors conducting research should use their data accurately and restrict their conclusions to those compatible with their methodology.

B.8 Resolving Conflicts between Ethical Priorities:

B.8.1 Counsellors will, from time to time, find themselves caught between conflicting ethical principles. In these circumstances, they are urged to consider the particular situation in which they find themselves and to discuss the situation with their counselling supervisor and/or other experienced counsellors. Even after conscientious consideration of the salient issues, some ethical dilemmas cannot be resolved easily or wholly satisfactorily.

B.8.2 Ethical issues may arise which have not yet been given full consideration. The Standards and Ethics Sub-Committee of this Association is interested in hearing of the ethical difficulties of counsellors, as helps to inform discussion regarding good practice.

B.9 The Availability of other Codes and Guidance Relating to Counselling:

B.9.1 The following codes and procedures have been passed by the Annual General Meeting of the British Association for Counselling:

Code of Ethics and Practice for Counselling Skills applies to members who would not regard themselves as counsellors, but who use counselling skills to support other roles.

Code of Ethics and Practice for the Supervision of Counsellors exists to guide members offering supervision to counsellors and to help counsellors seeking supervision.

Code of Ethics and Practice for Trainers in Counselling and Trainers in Counselling Skills exists to guide members offering training and to help members of the public seeking counselling training.

Complaints Procedure exists to guide members of BAC and their clients resolving complaints about breaches of the Codes of Ethics and Practice.

Copies and other guidelines and information sheets relevant to maintaining ethical standards of practice can be obtained from the BAC office, 1 Regent Place, Rugby CV21 2PJ.

Guidelines also available:

Telephone helplines: Guidelines for Good Practice is intended to establish standards for people working on telephone helplines (sponsored by British Telecom). Single copies available from Telephone Helplines Association, 61 Gray's Inn Road, London WC1X 8LT.

Notes and References

Chapter 1. Is Counsellor Training for You?

1. 'Is Counsellor Training for You?' is a weekend course run by Westminster Pastoral Foundation, 23 Kensington Square, London W8 5HN. Telephone 0171–937 6956.

Chapter 2. On Being a Counsellor

1. Psychodynamic training – this is the first of several counselling approaches mentioned by the counsellors in this chapter. These approaches are explained in Chapter 6.

Chapter 3. The Qualities of a Good Counsellor

1. *Gloria, Three Approaches to Psychotherapy*, Concord Video and Film Council, 201 Felixstowe Rd, Ipswich IP3 9BJ.
2. The list 'The Qualities of a Good Counsellor' is compiled from the responses of participants on the course 'Is Counsellor Training for You?' at Westminster Pastoral Foundation, February 1995.
3. *The Oxford Illustrated Dictionary*, Oxford University Press, 1984.
4. Charles Rycroft, *A Critical Dictionary of Psychoanalysis*, Penguin, 1972.
5. Patrick Casement, *On Learning from the Patient*, Tavistock, 1985.

Chapter 4. The Skills of a Good Counsellor

1. Joseph Weizenbaum, *ELIZA: A Computer Program for the Study of Natural Language Communication Between Man and Machine*, quoted in Margaret Boden, *Artificial Intelligence and Natural Man*, Open University Press, 1977, pp. 106–7.
2. Colby, Watt and Gilbert, *A Computer Method of Psychotherapy*, quoted in Boden, *Artificial Intelligence and Natural Man*, p. 60.
3. Virginia Axline, *Dibs: In Search of Self*, Pelican Books, 1971.
4. Sigmund Freud wrote about 'repetition compulsion' in *Beyond the Pleasure Principle*, J. Strachey (ed.), *The Complete Psychological Works of Sigmund Freud, vol. XVIII*, Hogarth Press, 1920.
5. Sheldon Kopp, *If You Meet the Buddha on the Road, Kill Him*, Sheldon Press, 1974, p. 2.

6. Henrik Ibsen, *A Doll's House, Ibsen Plays Two*, Methuen 'Master Playwrights' series, 1974.
7. Ibsen, *A Doll's House*, p. 98.
8. Frank L. Baum, *The Wizard of Oz*, Puffin, 1995.

Chapter 5. Knowing Yourself

1. Gerard Manley Hopkins, 'No worst, there is none', in *The Penguin Book of English Verse*, Penguin, 1956, p. 389.
2. Sigmund Freud, *The Interpretation of Dreams*, J. Strachey (ed.) *The Complete Psychological Works of Sigmund Freud, vol. XVIII*.

Chapter 6. Choosing an Approach

1. Frederick S. Perls, *Gestalt Therapy Verbatim*, quoted in Muriel James and Dorothy Jongeward, *Born to Win*, Signet, New York, 1978, p. 10.
2. Psychodynamic counselling – an introduction to the psychodynamic approach to counselling can be found in Michael Jacobs, *Psychodynamic Counselling in Action*, Sage Publications, 1988.
3. Psychoanalysis – for a fuller picture of Freud's life read: Richard Stephens, *Freud and Psychoanalysis*, Open University Press, 1983. For an introduction to Freud's ideas read: Sigmund Freud, *Introductory Lectures on Psychoanalysis*, vol. 1, Pelican, 1995. For a useful general introduction to psychoanalytic theory, with many examples from casework, read: Neville Symington, *The Analytic Experience*, Free Association Books, 1986.
4. Freud's case studies can be found in: Sigmund Freud, *Two Case Histories*, J. Strachey (ed.), *The Complete Psychological Works of Sigmund Freud, vol. X*, Hogarth Press, 1909, pp. 259–60.
5. For an introduction to Jung's life and ideas read: Carl G. Jung, *Memories, Dreams, Reflections*, Collins Fount Paperbacks, 1977.
6. For an introduction to Klein's life and ideas read: Hannah Segal, *Introduction to the Work of Melanie Klein*, Hogarth Press, 1973.
7. Behavioural counselling – an explanation of the behavioural approach to counselling can be found in: Joseph Wolpe, *The Practice of Behaviour Therapy* (Second Edition), Pergamon Press, 1973.
8. A history of early developments in behavioural theory, including the work of Pavlov and Watson, can be found in: Robert Boakes, *From Darwin to Behaviourism*, Cambridge University Press, 1984.

9. For an introduction to Skinner's ideas read: B. F. Skinner, *Science and Human Behaviour*, Collier-Macmillan, 1953.

10. For an introduction to Eysenck's ideas read: Hans J. Eysenck, *You and Your Neurosis*, Fontana/Collins, 1977.

11. See note 7 above.

12. M. E. Weishaar and Aaron T. Beck, 'Cognitive Therapy', in W. Dryden and W. Golden (eds) *Cognitive-Behavioural Approaches to Psychotherapy*, Harper and Row, 1986.

13. For a comprehensive account of social cognitive theory read: Albert Bandura, *Social Foundations of Thought and Action: A Social Cognitive Theory*, Prentice-Hall, 1986.

14. For an introduction to Albert Ellis' life and work read: Albert Ellis and Windy Dryden, *A Dialogue with Albert Ellis*, Open University Press, 1991.

15. For an introduction to rational-emotive behaviour counselling read: Windy Dryden, *Rational-Emotional Counselling in Action*, Sage Publications, 1990.

16. For an introduction to Aaron Beck's life and work read: M. E. Weishaar, *Aaron T. Beck*, Sage Publications, 1993.

17. For an introduction to existential philosophy read: Paul Tillich, *The Courage to Be*, Yale University Press, 1952.

18. For a powerful flavour of existential counselling in action read: Irving D. Yalom, *Love's Executioner and Other Tales of Psychotherapy*, Bloomsbury, 1989.

19. For introductions to the life and work of Rollo May, Irving Yalom and Viktor Frankl read: Richard Nelson-Jones, *The Theory and Practice of Counselling* (Second Edition), Cassell, 1995, pp. 114, 115, 135–6.

20. See note 19 above.

21. See note 19 above.

22. For an introduction to the theory and practice of existential counselling read: Emmy Van Deurzen-Smith, *Existential Counselling in Practice*, Sage, 1988.

23. For an introduction to the theory and practice of logotherapy read: Viktor E. Frankl, *The Will to Meaning*, Meridian, New York, 1969.

24. For Carl Rogers' account of his philosophy and counselling practice read: Carl R. Rogers, *Client-Centred Therapy*, Constable, 1951.

25. For theory and research on self-actualization read: A. H. Maslow, *Towards a Psychology of Being*, Van Nostrand, Princeton, New Jersey, 1962.

26. For Fritz Perls' autobiography read: F. S. Perls, *In and Out of the Garbage Pail*, Bantam, 1969.

27. For a comprehensive account of the theory and practice of gestalt counselling read: F. S. Perls, R. F. Hefferline and P. Goodman, *Gestalt Therapy*, Pelican Books, 1973.

28. The 'empty chair' technique is described in Muriel James and Dorothy Jongeward, *Born to Win*, Signet, New York, 1978, pp. 8–10.

29. For an edited transcript of audio-tapes of Fritz Perls' workshops read: F. R. Perls, *Gestalt Therapy Verbatim*, Bantam, 1971.

30. For an introduction to the life and work of Eric Berne read: I. Stewart, *Eric Berne*, Sage, 1992.

31. For a comprehensive account of the theory and practice of transactional analysis read: Eric Berne, *Transactional Analysis in Psychotherapy*, Evergreen, 1961; and Eric Berne, *Games People Play*, Penguin, 1968. See also James and Jongeward, *Born to Win*.

32. The British Association for Counselling, *Training in Counselling and Psychotherapy: A Directory*, obtainable from BAC, 1 Regent Place, Rugby, Warwickshire CV21 2PJ. Telephone 01788 550899.

Chapter 7. Choosing a Training

1. The British Association for Counselling, see Chapter 6, note 32.

2. Further information about the United Kingdom Register of Counsellors can be obtained from The Registrar, who has the same address as the BAC.

3. The Consortium of Scottish Counselling Organisations, 64 Murray Place, Stirling, FD8 2BX. Telephone 01786 475140.

4. Cruse – Bereavement Care, Cruse House, 126 Sheen Rd, Richmond TW9 1UR. Telephone 0181–940 4818.

5. Relate, Herbert Gray College, Little Church St, Rugby, Warwickshire CV21 3AP.

6. The Association for Pastoral Care and Counselling can be contacted through the BAC.

7. Westminster Pastoral Foundation, 23 Kensington Square, London W8 5HN. Telephone 0171–937 6956.

8. See Chapter 6, note 32.

9. For supervision requirements, see the BAC training directory, *Training in Counselling and Psychotherapy: A Directory*, p. ix.

10. The British Psychological Society, St Andrews House, 48 Princes Rd East, Leicester LE1 7DR.

11. The BAC *Code of Ethics and Practice for Counsellors* is to be found in full in the Appendix.

12. The United Kingdom Council for Psychotherapy, 167–169 Great Portland St, London W1N 5FB.

13. The British Confederation of Psychotherapists, 37 Mapesbury Rd. London NW2 4HJ.

Chapter 8. Practising Counselling

1. Notes are from the 'Guidelines for client work, training placements and supervision in counsellor training courses', devised by the BAC Scheme for the Recognition of Counsellor Training Courses. They were first published in *Counselling* (the journal of BAC), in February 1996, pp. 5–7.
2. The BAC *Code of Ethics and Practice for Counsellors* is to be found in full in the Appendix.
3. For a useful introduction to this area of counselling practice read: Patricia East, *Counselling in Medical Settings*, Open University Press, 1995.
4. For a useful introduction to this area of counselling practice read: *Counselling Skills and Counselling at Work*, The Association for Counselling at Work, obtainable from BAC.
5. Elsa Bell, *Counselling in Further and Higher Education*, Open University Press, 1996.
6. Information on the criteria to be met by applicants for BAC trainer accreditation can be obtained from BAC. For the address, see Chapter 6, note 32.
7. The BAC *Code of Ethics and Practice for Counsellors*, Clause B.4.8. The code is to be found in full in the Appendix.
8. Details of the Data Protection Act are available from the Office of the Data Protection Registrar, Wycliffe House, Water Lane, Wilmslow, Cheshire SK9 5AF.
9. Information sheets on supervision and other aspects of counselling practice are obtainable from the publications department of BAC. A catalogue will be sent on request. BAC, 1 Regent Place, Rugby, Warwickshire, CV21 2PJ. Telephone 01788 550899.
10. For an introduction to the life and work of D. W. Winnicott read: Madeleine Davis and David Wallbridge, *Boundary and Space*, H. Karnak Books Ltd., 1981.

Further Reading

Most of the relevant books are listed in the Notes and References section. The list which follows contains other titles which I have found to be useful to students of counselling skills and counselling. This is a very personal list. These are all books which have set me thinking beyond the obvious.

Acheson, F. and Lake, T., *Counselling Listener*, The National Extension College, 1990. An introduction to counselling designed as an interactive course, with a handbook and audio-tapes.

Appignanesi, R. and Zarate, O., *Freud for Beginners*, Icon Books, 1992. One in an intriguing series (there is also a book on Jung in the series). The books have a comic strip format, but you should not assume that they are simplistic. This volume explains Freud's life and his theoretical development clearly and effectively.

Coltart, N., *How to Survive as a Psychotherapist*, Sheldon Press, 1993. This is a fascinating and readable account of the life and work of a therapist, written by a very experienced, highly respected practitioner.

Dryden, W. (ed.), *Individual Therapy in Britain*, Harper and Row, 1984.

Guggenbuhl-Craig, A., *Power in the Helping Professions*, Spring Publications Inc., Dallas, Texas, 1971. A thought-provoking book about the challenges of working in a 'helping' profession and the dangers of therapists abusing their power.

Jacobs, M., *The Presenting Past*, Harper and Row, 1985. 'An introduction to practical psychodynamic counselling', to quote the subtitle.

Laing, R. D., *Knots*, Penguin, 1972. Poetry written by an unorthodox psychiatrist and his team to help them to 'unwind'. Thought-provoking insights into neurotic thoughts and feelings.

Nelson-Jones, R., *The Theory and Practice of Counselling* (Second Edition), Cassell, 1995.

Phillips, A., *On Kissing, Tickling and Being Bored*, Faber and Faber, 1993. Who could resist a book with such an intriguing title? Adam Phillips is a psychoanalyst. In this book of essays he asks himself and us intriguing questions about the human condition.

Skynner, R. and Cleese. J., *Families and How to Survive Them*, Methuen, 1983. Robin Skynner, family therapist, and John Cleese, comedian and recipient of therapy, look at the development of relationships. The cartoon illustrations are a delight, and this book gets to grips with serious issues in an accessible way.

| *Index*